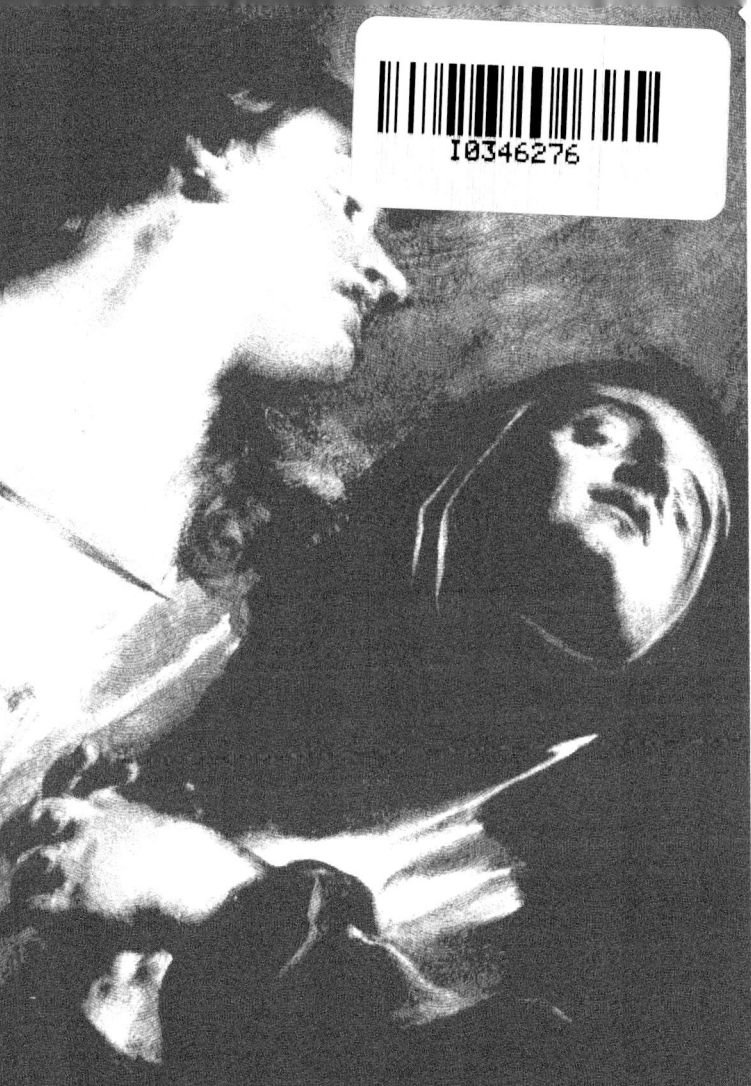

GEORGES BATAILLE: AN EPITOME
LYNN HUGHEY ENGELBERT

KISMET PRESS
EPITOMES I | MMXVII

Georges Bataille

AN EPITOME

Lynn Hughey Engelbert

kısmet·press

Libera Scientia | Free Knowledge

Georges Bataille: An Epitome
by Lynn Hughey Engelbert

Epitomes, 1
Series Editors: Tim Barnwell & N. Kıvılcım Yavuz

Published in 2017
by Kismet Press LLP
15 Queen Square, Leeds, LS2 8AJ, UK
kismet.press
kismet@kismet.press

Copyright © 2017 Lynn Hughey Engelbert

Published by Kismet Press LLP under an exclusive license to publish. Commercial copying, hiring, lending is prohibited. The book is freely available online at <kismet.press> under a Creative Commons Attribution-NonCommercial-NoDerivatives 4.0 International (CC BY-NC-ND 4.0) license. See <https://creativecommons.org/licenses/by-nc-nd/4.0/> for details.

Downloadable .epub edition also available

Printed and bound by IngramSpark with acid-free paper, using a print-on-demand model with printers in the US, EU, and Australia

A catalogue record for this book is available from the British Library

ISBN 978-0-9956717-3-7 (pbk)
ISBN 978-0-9956717-4-4 (ebk)

Contents

I	An Introduction: Georges Bataille and Impossibility	1
II	The General and Restricted Economies: Outsider Philosophy	13
III	Sovereignty, Transgression, and Power: Bataille's Subject	29
IV	Transgression, Art, and Surrealism: In-between the Avant-Garde and Literature	45
V	Outsider Literature(s) inside the Abyss	59
VI	The Sacred/Profane or Eroticism/Ecstasy: Saint Bataille	89
VII	A Conclusion for Bataille and the Anti-Aesthetic	115
	Bibliography	127
	Credits	133

I
An Introduction: Georges Bataille and Impossibility

THIS INTRODUCTION TO GEORGES BATAILLE'S WORK IS first, an identification of *impossibility* as a key theme throughout his writing/life, and second, a kind of radical overturning of the traditional structures of rational philosophy in *reading* his work and his life. He was, undoubtedly, an impossible philosopher, offering radically different philosophical works that were resistant to the interests of mainstream philosophy. And as well, he was an author of the impossible; an avant-garde author of literary works that were provocative and resistant to literary interpretation (or "pornological").[1] Together these two forms of impossibility allowed Bataille to merge literature and philosophy in structural narratives and theoretical treatises characterized by excess, complexity, and transgression. So here, I think that the most important thing to consider is the way that *impossibility*, once identified in these two ways, allows for a *possible* reading or understanding of Bataille, in an(other) kind of relationship.

Without the prior condition of possibility, impossibility in Bataille could not be manifested; as he suggested in his introduction to the *Theory of Religion*, the "ensemble" of all the structural elements of a book, work, and the "whole human assemblage and edifice," is the tradition of possibility. Yet every work displaces this as well, because "the unlimited assemblage is the impossible" and at "the apex of possibility, or at least awareness of the impossibility" consciousness "opens to all that it is possible to think."[2] In this introduction and throughout each of the primary sections in this text, I would appeal to the reader to maintain a recognition of *impossibility* yet *possibility* with Bataille's work, and to persist in the project of rendering an open space of reflection upon the evolution of both transgression and excess. The importance of reading Bataille in this way is what Carolyn Bailey Gill suggests is the possibility of understanding his work by way of "relations between politics, literature, and art" because, as she writes:

> Bataille is becoming unavoidable for anyone interested in contemporary debates on the concept of alterity, on the notion of the subject, on the nature of community, on the

relationship between representation and a particular theory of language.³

I argue that what Gill describes as unavoidability is even stronger in today's theoretical and critical landscape of postmodern malaise. I would also advise that a strong recognition of two things in relation to materialism is required for Bataille's reader: first, the idea that a "kind of mysticism" exists in "perversion"; like a "black theology" which inspires as a renunciation, yet is conditional on an original moment of theological affirmation. And second, that this "profound mystery" is one found in repetition as a "terrible force," yet a powerful aesthetic, as well.⁴ Together, these combine to offer the transgressive and excessive moments of transcendence/ruin that create a fascination for Bataille's work.

A brief biographical overview is necessary to begin: Georges Bataille was born in 1897 and died in 1962 in Reims, France, where his blind father, paralyzed and syphilitic, complicated his early childhood development. In 1915, during the First World War, as the Germans approached Reims, Bataille and his mother abandoned his insane father, who died shortly afterwards.⁵ Raised and schooled as a Catholic, Bataille's preoccupation with religion and Catholicism more specifically persisted throughout his life.

Bataille's early schooling as a "medievalist librarian" at the *École des Chartes* led to his position as such at the *Bibliothèque Nationale* in Paris, which he held until 1942. This professional position gave him a reliance upon taxonomy and order, yet at the same time, the basis for his refutation of these practices and epistemology.[6] The "double" life he led in Paris produced the writing which is now his most infamous signifier: and this from the foundation of what was a superficially moderate career and social presence.

In Bataille's adult life, various influences which proved to be the strongest in French intellectual/aesthetic and German philosophical history were always present in his work and thoughts: Surrealism and André Breton, Michel Leiris and Sade, as well as Nietzsche, Hegel, Marx, Darwin, and Marcel Mauss are all figures that haunt his writing, thinking, and philosophy. Allan Stoekl describes these influences as akin to an evolutionary progression for Bataille. First, there are a series of stages from the prehistoric or primordial moment of Lascaux, to a "parodic Nietzschean superman," and next, a fall of the "psychoanalytic cure" into the Hegelian dialectic; "toward Absolute Spirit."[7] This becomes finalized in what Stoekl sees as the ultimate post-evolutionary stage, for Bataille:

> at the *end* of reason, at the *end* of man, at the end of the Cartesian pineal gland (the supposed seat of consciousness) there is only orgasm and a simultaneous fall, [or] a simultaneous death.[8]

This double termination, characterized by death and/or perversion, is consistently generated and sustained by the "energy of the obscene," or the transgressive and destructive elements of Eros and Thanatos. Here,

Bataille's philosophy becomes based on the instinct of the animal alone, and all knowledge becomes non-knowledge, and therefore, all "humanity is animality; insight is blindness; health is terminal pathology" writes Stoekl.[9] In a literal reaction against middle-class or modern "sterile bourgeois society," Bataille used sacrifice, ecstasy, and excess to counter the rational and collective calmness of such a social homogeneity. For Bataille, there is no escape by way of transcendence via rational idealism, because everything is only known in an impossible relation with materialism that "does not pass beyond matter in the construction of a 'scientific' conceptual edifice," but instead "posits a matter that cannot be reduced to systems" of any nature: whether philosophical, political, or scientific.[10]

Incorporated into his theory of "expenditure"[11] is Bataille's reconceptualization of Hegel's negative dialectic into "nonabstract negativity," one which is commonly identified in the middle-class struggle for revolution, and this by way of "potlach," as a "destructive orgiastic drive" from Marcel Mauss as a force that becomes a loss without limit, or a "principle of loss [...] of unconditional expenditure."[12] Destruction acts as a reaffirmation of another kind of hierarchy against the bourgeois, and the ideal of revolution in this oscillation "is a liberation of the true nature of expenditure" which uses expenditure as a means toward revolt, finally allowing for "negativity put [be put] to work" or to produce by way of destruction.[13] This "sovereign form" of heterogeneity is created by the radicalization of homogeneity in its final stage, however, even as Bataille notes, the ability of such destructive transgression can, and does, power the success of fascist regimes, with the rise of the charismatic leader in conjunction with the orgiastic frenzy of the mob, and it employs reactionary forces of affectation as its most destructive yet persuasive power. Many events in human history exemplify this Dionysian, orgiastic expenditure in its brutal and uncontained manifestations. This is the ideal for, yet the ruin of the collective/communal vision Bataille offered, but as he would argue, this power unleashed is effectively mediated by the individual theory of sovereignty.

This individualistic version of heterogeneity and transgression in Bataille focused on Sade, because he was a "sovereign writer" who examined "the problem of eroticism and its eccentric yet powerful relation to human existence."[14] When Sade's monstrous philosophy and/or literature became the basis for Bataille's sovereignty, there occurred a "glorious expenditure as the possibility for a mingling of the most sacred and the unspeakably profane" by way of a "common transgression of the restricted economy of utility," argues Jane Gallop. This was a "natural" commingling of excess from Sade with Bataille's "hyper-masculine hero" or narrator.[15] This male presence and power in Bataille's novels always situated woman as an Other to this control, and women provided the energy and excess for material transgression to take on a form. In *Madame Edwarda*, *My Mother*, "Filthy," and *Story of the Eye* are found unpredictable, masochistic women characters that serve as the engines that drive both the male narrator's interest and fall, because of their feminine alterity.

For Gilles Deleuze, the "pornological literature" in Bataille's novels offers the reader a "dual language" out of these two energies,[16] and it adheres to stereotypical features of such literature because it confronts the external façade of the text's surface

> with its own limits, with what is in a sense a "non-language" (violence that does not speak, eroticism that remains unspoken).[17]

And next, the internal splitting of language occurs because of "the imperative and descriptive function" of the text becoming dislocated.[18] The paradox of masochism which drives this duality is one that Bataille identified as "essentially that of a victim."[19] But this is also the impossibility of language in the depiction of violence: Bataille described this violence in opposition to civilized humanity,[20] and texts which determine this sadistic/masochistic violence cannot communicate literally but do so via the victim's demise or suffering. The "demonstration is identical to violence" yet it is not, as it is a "mere reflection of a higher form of violence to which the demonstration [and masochist] testifies."[21]

Neither Sade nor Bataille's work fits a traditional aim or presentation of pornography and as Karmen MacKendrick argues, as pornography, this form of writing "is a series of failures" because Sade's texts use language that is "too clinical," "overloaded" with "machines and philosophy lectures," and overly "violent beyond any pornographic possibility."[22] In Bataille and Sade, the reader will not find a clear pornographic climax, and I would argue that

MacKendrick's analysis of Sade is also perfectly suited to Bataille as follows:

> It is form that fascinates—but, like Sade, we find ourselves most profoundly drawn by the moment of form's self-inversion or destruction, by its autotransgressive aspects.[23]

In a broader sense, Bataille's work fits within a subcategorical evolutionary and theoretical space, between structuralism and poststructuralism, and this is a form of "antihumanism" which seeks to reverse the tenets of humanist philosophy, morality, and literature. Communication, representation, and aesthetic relations are all disrupted, and in both Sade and Bataille antihumanist concerns are used to deflate philosophical questions of a metaphysical nature. This is/was a "movement to contaminate philosophy" with the messy, unpredictable, and irrational material of the world, Gallop wrote, and in distinctly antihumanist circles such as those that housed Foucault, Barthes, Deleuze, Lacan, and Derrida, as well as more contemporary postmoderns.

I would argue this remains an *anti-philosophical* history into a post-postmodernity, as well.[24] André Breton's *Mad Love* (although someone/something that Bataille would reject most thoroughly here), is an interesting correspondent to this aesthetic rejection of the rational, and Breton's "convulsive beauty" offers a singular example to see how this order is contested: "Convulsive beauty will be veiled-erotic, fixed-explosive, magic-circumstantial, or it will not be."[25] And as is true of Bataille, radical materialism is the vehicle for this aesthetic ideal: "*chance* is the form making manifest the exterior necessity which traces its path in the human consciousness" argues Breton of "modern materialists."²⁶ The tension between the singular, sovereign subject, and the force of the transgressive community in Bataille's work, however attractive or intriguing, is one that cannot allow for any consensual or harmonious consistency, such as democracy or universal humanism. This new conception of community creates and sustains the conflict between the individual's freedom and the restrictions on the most radically situated group, such as the *Acéphale*.

Breton's description of "sympathy existing between two or several beings" offers an accessory account to the complexity in Bataille, and the circumstantial or "accidental" are the events that bring about a "second finality, in the sense of the possible reaching of some goal by the lining of our will," or the commingling of "suffering."²⁷ This also sustains a variety of disruptions in the Political and the Social, which allow transgression to effectively destroy positive manifestations in either sphere. So, if there are two key metaphors that exist for Bataille's ideal of the sovereign man and the transgressive expenditure of the community, it would be the solitary Sadean libertine who moves inside and outside of the text, as well as the headless, acephalic man who is a/all member(s) of the heterogeneous community in its delirium. And like Breton, who credits Sade with inventing the "sublime imagination, linked to the philosophical conscience" because for Sade, "man no longer unites with nature except in crime," Bataille follows a similar kind of reflective path. This impossibility of harmony between communal and individual existence, or human/Nature, is the basis for Bataille's literature and/or philosophical works, and the "rupture of unity through a rewriting of 'major' philosophies" is "a resolutely marginal, fragmentary, and impossible project."[28] Breton's position is more akin to Bataille than different in regards to such a project:

> The child I still am in relation to what I should like to be has not quite unlearned the dualism of good and evil. These roots, half in the air, half under the ground, these vines, these indiscernible snakes, this mixture or seduction and fear.[29]

In this book, I will offer a critical deconstruction of the philosophical theories of Bataille's general and restricted economies of "outsider" philosophy more generally for Chapter 2, and follow in Chapter 3 with an examination of sovereignty, transgression, and power as central foundations for Bataille's philosophical theories. In Chapter 4, the relationship between Surrealism, art, aesthetics, and sacrifice are primary areas I will analyze accordingly, followed by an introduction to Bataille's transgressive approach to literature in Chapter 5. In Chapters 6 and 7, I will provide a complex, critical reading of the profane and the sacred in terms of dualistic forms of what is finally, in the conclusion (Chapter 8), an open kind of resolution to this introduction to Bataille's work. The understanding of the "open wound," the "desire for the other," and "sacrifice" is Bataille's "objection to a complete rationality dreamed by the philosophers" argues Jean-Michel Besnier.[30] "Confronting in herself, the feeling of being," a "savage impossibility," always seeking transgression of the limits of existence, writes Besnier.[31]

The reader is never unaffected by Bataille's work or the gaps it opens in terms of thought, and the excess of pleasure, transgression, and suffering is always a "*savage form of enjoyment*," writes MacKendrik, between the asceticism of possibility and impossible readings of something outside of this, I will conclude.[32] The search for the "divine life" is something that "requires that the seeker after it shall die."[33]

Notes

1. Deleuze, 17.
2. Bataille, *Theory of Religion*, 9–10.
3. Gill, xix.
4. Deleuze, 104–105.
5. Stoekl, "Introduction," in *Visions of Excess*, ix.
6. Stoekl, "Introduction," in *Visions of Excess*, x.
7. Stoekl, "Introduction," in *Visions of Excess*, xii.
8. Stoekl, "Introduction," in *Visions of Excess*, xii.
9. Stoekl, "Introduction," in *Visions of Excess*, xiii.
10. Stoekl, "Introduction," in *Visions of Excess*, xv.
11. Bataille, "Notion of Expenditure," 1933.
12. Bataille, *Visions of Excess*, 118.
13. Stoekl, "Introduction," in *Visions of Excess*, xvi–xvii.
14. Gallop, 7.

15 Gallop, 11–12.
16 Deleuze, 19.
17 Deleuze, 21.
18 Deleuze, 21.
19 Bataille qtd. in Deleuze, 16.
20 Bataille, *Literature and Evil*, 191.
21 Deleuze, 18.
22 MacKendrick, 29.
23 MacKendrick, 32–33.
24 Gallop, 3–4.
25 Breton, 19.
26 Breton, 23.
27 Breton, 34–35.
28 Stoekl, "Introduction," in *Visions of Excess*, xxi.
29 Breton, 76.
30 Besnier, 20.
31 Besnier, 20.
32 MacKendrik, 65.
33 Bataille qtd. in MacKendrik, 73.

II
The General and Restricted Economies: Outsider Philosophy

IN BATAILLE'S ECONOMIC THEORY OF EXPENDITURE and energetic translation, there is a dualism which provides the foundation for an either/or paradox concerning human nature and society, and this complex binary relationship creates the possibility of human resistance in the face of homogeneity/conformity or all things "economic." The argument he offers concerning heterogeneity qualifies his philosophical approach to human, psychological, and natural kinds of economies as an outsider's account, mainly because the outcome of this oppositional approach to an ordered analysis arises out of alterity and produces a radical form of difference. The political is therefore the economic for Bataille, but only as it originates from the psychological or libidinal excess of Freudian desire and the existential refusal of normativity.

This critique of a dichotomy between what is mainstream and/or subversive is something that Jean Piel identifies in Bataille's work from "The Notion of Expenditure" to *The Accursed Share*, as an "attempt at representing the world," or "a sort of essay on universal History."[1] The concept of "unproductive expenditure" is a cornerstone for a broader consideration of natural and human determination for Bataille, a theory that extends into aesthetics, the social, the political, and the psychoanalytical argues Piel, and he positioned this excess within subjective experiences of individual "eroticism and anguish."[2] For example, in "The Notion of Expenditure," the groundwork for an analysis of "utility" is framed by an evaluation of material usefulness or "classical utility" in opposition to "pleasure," and both are reduced or constrained by material capitalism and reproduction for Bataille.[3] The humanism that underlies the "right to acquire, to conserve, and to consume rationally" is a social and political one, and it is based on the economic order of homogeneity that pushes aside "nonproductive expenditure" argues Bataille.[4]

Towards expanding this position, he first proposes the "principle of loss" as being a primary theoretical imperative, as expenditure always implies a loss as "unconditional expenditure" is illustrated by the following examples: jewels are never as valuable as they appear, and are "useless," and as well, cults which enact sacrifice and consume or expend a sacred object without gain of any material consequence.[5] Bataille declares that loss is also a fact of material life, like sustenance and/or evacuation, and these are compared to the loss in spending money or extravagance with such funds.[6] And artistic production, which is architectural construction, as well as "symbolic expenditure" (including poetry) is the best example of "creation by means of a loss" for Bataille.[7] The utility of the poet's work is always questionable, especially from the perspective of a rational order, he argues. From here, he describes production, exchange, and activity that is inherently "unproductive" in another set of expenditures: production is always seen by way of the dominant order's wealth and status, with the change occurring through violent, social expenditure, and exchange is therefore seen in its archaic form as the "potlach," where the gift is an open assertion of rivalry and obligation. When the potlatch combines with "religious sacrifice," the destruction of wealth is the end game. Therefore, it is only "through loss that glory and honor are linked to wealth" argues Bataille, and the potlatch is unproductive expenditure.[8] These are "expenditures of an antagonistic type," and not exchanges.[9]

For Bataille, both bourgeois possession and accumulation of wealth underlies this "sinister cancellation" of human existence, providing restraints for expenditure "in conformity with a reasoning that balances *accounts*."[10] *The Accursed Share* rearticulated these earlier analyses of expenditure for Bataille and as Piel suggests, the new version was an attempt

> to put together a systematic exposé of his vision of the world—a philosophy of nature, a

philosophy of man, a philosophy of economy, a philosophy of history.[11]

In *The Accursed Share* Bataille also identifies the mechanisms of consumption which are created by excessive wealth, and the sovereign subject's desires, and this is exemplified within the general realm of "exudation (of waste) of living matter," which allows for this subject's impulse towards "useless consumption."[12] The second consideration which Bataille examines is the desire for such excess materiality, which first exists in the "poverty of the organism," one that creates this excess inside a limited system such as an economy (generalized).[13] Class struggle reasserts the excess or inessential nature of the heterogeneous moment of desire entering the system, reforming the ruling class by revolutionary means, and the result is that the slave rises up to defeat the master, and revolution "answers the unlimited demands of the masses" against the "contemptuous forms that exclude human nature."[14] Here, his idea of the "*economy* of the universe" is a pinning of the donkey's tail on either production or expenditure, or, more fully, "what *crime* represents in relation to the law" as an "insubordinate characterization."[15]

In *The Accursed Share*, the "Preface" contains the most interesting remarks from Bataille concerning value, loss, and expenditure. He describes how he

> had a point of view from which a human sacrifice, the construction of a church or the

gift of a jewel were no less interesting than the sale of wheat.[16]

The range of his concern given here, the "excess energy, translated into the effervescence of life," was broader than an economist's view, and incorporated art, literature, and poetry into this capitalist system, without an objective distance, and with great personal investment or interest.[17] He writes: "everything is rich—in other words, everything that is commensurate with the universe" and free, as well, formed from a free mind and a "lucid attitude."[18] But briefly, I think that the idea of consumption here remains codependent on production and nature (and humans), and this causes this economic disruption to occur in a cyclical way, as creation and destruction co-exist, apart from the specific nature of the distinct economies themselves. Bataille argues that it may be that humanity "exploits given material resources with restriction," and then consumes them as a pursuit of "the useless and infinite fulfillment of the universe."[19] But a basic truism remains: the "living organism" ends up receiving "more energy than is necessary for sustaining life," and therefore, growth occurs, and once this growth has reached its limit, the excess cannot be subsumed or spent. It is clear that this excess creates a body of expenditure that must be consumed in some manner, whether "gloriously or catastrophically."[20] And as can be seen in the accumulation of excess wealth or material goods in small or large scale considerations, or the enterprise of war as compelled by the "excesses of life force," when its rationalization of expansion overrides humanist ethics, it is the combination of aggression and overabundance that create these distinct occurrences.[21]

This provides Bataille with a foundation to examine the restricted nature of this excessive energy as it is opposed to, yet interdependent with the general economy. The material principles of growth involve pressure (as is seen in the material limits of the world which create this as a struggle for existence in Darwin), and this complies with a theory of life as expansion; one that is contained (limited), yet overwhelms utility.[22] The compression, and next, the explosion of this energy occurs when pressure is released, and this is evident in death (organic) and destruction (revolution or war) or expansion (broadening a space in territorial conflict).[23]

For Bataille, all material life exhibits "a luxurious squandering of energy in every form," and the "history of life on earth is mainly the effect of a wild exuberance," as is best seen in something akin to the Dionysian revel I would argue.[24] This is largely unconscious in its movement, so the "accursed share" is the obvious result: where both the "explosive character of the world" conjoins with "the explosive tension" of human life (death, eating and consumption in general, reproduction and libidinal excess) to fulfill the conditions of something akin to a Big Bang, I would assert.[25] The "accursed share" is "a curse" which "weighs on human life," one that can only be lifted by a kind of mass enlightenment of human consciousness. Bataille sees this as only being possible when the "avoidance of the truth [that] ensures, in reciprocal fashion, a recognition of the truth," occurs, but the truth here is only the "general economy" itself, or conformity which appears on the surface of heterogeneity.[26] The elements that are necessary for radical Otherness only emerge in what is group or community consumption and/or violence. He describes this as follows: "consumption is the way in which *separate* beings communicate" and this allows "everything" to be "open and infinite between those who consume intensely," because "violence is released and it breaks forth without limits" to affect those who are consumed.[27] "Sacrifice" is the main manifestation of this violence, and scapegoating allows the community to be saved from ruin as the "*victim* is given over to violence."[28] The victim is therefore, "a surplus taken from the mass of useful wealth" and it is an excess which is "consumed profitlessly, and therefore utterly destroyed" in this process. The victim is also the symbolic representation of the "accursed share, destined for violent consumption," argues Bataille.[29] Finally, the victim acts as this curse's "recognizable figure," someone who "radiates intimacy, anguish, the profundity of living beings," and represents every person, yet is only one.[30]

This economic set of tensions allows Bataille to move into a naturalized or determinate consideration of human desire and constraint, as the individual remains a reflection of the group, nation, or species, and is composed of, yet subject to, the symbiotic relationship between expenditure and/or generation. This relation is strained, as s/he is also subject to economies of conformity and/or radical alterity. The central claim that Bataille offers in regards to the economic energy of immanence is the way that the sacrifice of the individual is inherent in the concept of the gift or the "potlach," and for this he describes the traditional article of exchange not as a mere "thing," but as a symbol of rivalry and wealth on the part of the giver; the earmark of aggression.[31] It is like commerce, "a means of circulating wealth, but it excludes bargaining."[32] It creates obligation and rivalry in terms of the power it represents/possesses, and in being repaid, the gift is usually not so much an exchange as an event of one-upmanship. Bataille suggests that "the ideal would be that a potlatch could not be repaid."[33] But potlatch always involves rank, status, and aggression based upon the stark contrast between wealth and poverty, and it is always those who are "poverty-stricken" that reject this form of gift and acquisition from the wealthy. The gift is "based on the principle of exchange" in an individual/cultural sense, and its status within a "vast network of rites, celebrations, contracts and rivalries" that organize "the mechanics of these transactions."[34]

This "expense" or value of the gift is a "manifestation both religious and social," and is a "pure loss."[35] Rodolphe Gasché describes Marcel Mauss' conception of the gift as a "reflection of ethnology upon itself, to its destruction," and his essay "On The Gift" as "a project for the reduction and appropriation of submission to form and reason."[36] This "pure expenditure" of the gift, later seen in Bataille's heterogeneous economic function, leads to a "displacement," argues Gasché, and cannot be mapped onto present-day systems of "avarice," allowing it to be "denounced as a pure effect" despite the antagonism which always underlies the "idea of reciprocity" in the traditional potlatch.[37] Pierre Bourdieu argues that only "agents endowed with dispositions adjusted to the logic of 'disinterestedness'" (dispositions that can culminate in the "supreme sacrifice," or "giving one's life," or "dying for the fatherland") can participate in the potlatch, as Bataille describes it.[38] These are people who have a

> complete contempt for riches, like the somber indifference of the individual who refuses work and makes his life on the one hand, an infinitely ruined splendor, and on the other, a silent insult to the laborious lie of the rich

and these things exemplify the individual's "exuberance to revolt."[39] Bourdieu describes these people as those who can suspend the gift economy by way of "the collective denial of the economic foundations of human existence."[40] In both descriptions, the proletariat are no doubt a model. Nonetheless, the economy of the gift is always problematic because it is based "on the opposition between passion and interest," as well as "constraint and freedom, individual choice and collective pressure, disinterestedness and self-interest."[41]

Bataille's use of this "gift economy" opposes the tenets of capitalist society and, therefore, it is intrinsically political. Against the backdrop of communism in the U.S.S.R. and American industrialization, militarism, religion, and economic capitalism, Bataille became concerned with the alterity of conscious/unconscious energies as they were manifested in his theory of general and restricted economies. The comparison he makes between Buddhism (and Lamaism) as being grounded in peaceful and powerless forms of "revolt," and Islamic religious militarism,[42] exemplifies the way that a philosophical doctrine such as Buddhism is "the opposite of the other systems: it avoids activity, which is always directed towards acquisition and growth," and "it ceases [...] to subject life to any other ends but life itself: Directly and immediately, life is its own end."[43] This revolutionary approach

> confronts human activity within its limits, and describes—beyond military or productive activity—a world that is unsubordinated by any necessity.[44]

For Bataille, this also opposes the religious forms of influence in the jihadism of radical Islamic movements (military societies), as well as the Lutheran (Protestant) character of communist nations in general, and finally, the modern, industrial, social structures since the Reformation, such as those seen in the U.S. (the Marshall Plan is Bataille's focus here).

The juxtaposition of specific forms and a general, historical overview leads to a conclusion that the "choice that people of today will make regarding the mode for expending unavoidable excess—this choice will determine their future."[45] And rather than undergoing explosive and violent expenditure, if they choose to "bring about" this surplus in energetic or positive ways, there could be a refusal of the curse, or the explicit rejection of the destructive nature of unregulated and unconscious desire (the mob). Nonetheless, it still seems to be a choice between two oppositional extremes: on the one hand, "to let the surplus provoke more and more catastrophic explosions rather than 'consuming' it," or as Piel suggests, "consciously destroying it through ways they can choose and 'agree to.'"[46] For Piel, Bataille's examination of the Marshall Plan "awakens" a degree of "hope" in the final chapters of *The Accursed Share*, as it seeks to use a "doomed wealth in order to open up new possibilities for growth" throughout the world.[47] In a prophetic manner, Piel sees Bataille's work here as an "illumination" which foretells the "paradoxical changes" between "Soviet and American events at the end of the 1950s" as concrete developments. These paradoxical tensions prophesized the Cold War:

> the growing waste of atomic and space-rated expenditures of the two greatest world powers could appear one day, like a giant *potlach*, as though they were the means of avoiding more or less consciously, "that catastrophic expenditure of excess energy" that is war.[48]

Piel writes,

> Thus in *The Accursed Share*, Georges Bataille, a precursor of the theory of the gift in modern economic life and of "generalized economy," was also—more than ten years before his time—the prophet of "peaceful coexistence" and of unexpected developments of the competition for expansion between two blocs.[49]

Allan Stoekl also sees Bataille's *Accursed Share* as prophetic in yet another way. In setting out the connections between the social "and the sacred,"[50] it was predictive of an end of history where humans do not cease to be entirely, but are more likely to become "animals."[51] This is a "return, but on a higher level, to the animality, the mere physical experience" that Kojève sees in Bataille's work. These animal/humans as "Posthistorical people will be dandies," says Stoekl.[52] And "dandyism" occurs within a "world of mutual recognition," a reality which is oriented around the gift, and it introduces "the arbitrary, the gratuitous, the pointless, [and] the excessive."[53] This creates conditions characterized by "confrontation, [and] defiance," and for Bataille, the dandy becomes "the madman, the lover," or the exemplary model for the sovereign subject.[54] This is best illustrated in the Marshall Plan says Stoekl, with the death of the "bourgeois individual" and the extension of the Soviet worker as the remaining subject, one who works to develop the State, a model which opposes that of "American *excess*."[55] The Marshall Plan reconfigures the Soviet model to be "one of conservation and recuperation," while the American "is one of expenditure without return."[56] For Stoekl the echoes of the potlatch are evident: The Americans

> are spending like the Tlingit chiefs of the American Northwest, without [...] any thought for the future, any plans for later construction or return.[57]

Further, it is valid to consider how Bataille's sovereign subject, "recognizes the Soviet 'slave'" as a "profound necessity and human labor," so it is clear that the sovereign subject does not "go beyond" the slave, as the slave has mastered the master, because this subject transgresses yet affirms the preconditional necessity of the proletariat, argues Stoekl.[58] Therefore, *The Accursed Share* is/is not a "classic cold war document," first, because it would need to provide "a rationale for political and economic policy of capitalist nations in the face of Communism," but second, it does this without valorizing a new capitalist bourgeois, because the human is "a symptom of cultural decadence, doomed and irrelevant" in Bataille's estimation.[59] It "doesn't describe the 'defeat of the Soviet Union,'" but it does describe the "Soviet threat" as a logical consequence of the general and restricted economies in human civilization.[60] For Bataille, the vast, collective potlatch exemplified here, functions as an "industrialized, collective dépense," as an expenditure that becomes "an intellectual and moral potlatch," and one that is inseparable from atheistic and "mystical experience" as opposed to pragmatic and economic "discourse," concludes Stoekl.[61] If one considers Jacques Derrida's estimation, this is the mark of a more general "différance" in the interpolation of the general and restricted economies where "the very project of philosophy" is "displaced and reinscribed."[62]

If the reader can respond to *The Accursed Share* as a kind of historical and anthropological philosophy concerning human nature, anguish, and history, or alternately, a re-reading of human history between nations and economies, Bataille's strength in terms of this theory of the general and restricted economies (and the result of expenditure and/or surplus) is a compelling, interdisciplinary work. In this way, *The Accursed Share* is an account of many factors from the perspective of a radically different philosophy and/or philosopher, I conclude, and is equally difficult yet illuminating, as a result.

Notes

1 Piel, 97.
2 Piel, 99.
3 Bataille, *Visions of Excess*, 116–117.
4 Bataille, *Visions of Excess*, 117.
5 Bataille, *Visions of Excess*, 119.
6 Bataille, *Visions of Excess*, 119.
7 Bataille, *Visions of Excess*, 120.
8 Bataille, *Visions of Excess*, 121–122.
9 Bataille, *Visions of Excess*, 123.
10 Bataille, *Visions of Excess*, 124.
11 Piel, 101–102.
12 Bataille, *The Accursed Share*, 23.
13 Bataille, *The Accursed Share*, 22.
14 Bataille, *The Accursed Share*, 127.
15 Bataille, *The Accursed Share*, 129.
16 Bataille, *The Accursed Share*, 9.
17 Bataille, *The Accursed Share*, 10.
18 Bataille, *The Accursed Share*, 13–14.
19 Bataille, *The Accursed Share*, 21.
20 Bataille, *The Accursed Share*, 21.

21 Bataille, *The Accursed Share*, 24–25.
22 Bataille, *The Accursed Share*, 30–31.
23 Bataille, *The Accursed Share*, 32–33.
24 Bataille, *The Accursed Share*, 33.
25 Bataille, *The Accursed Share*, 40.
26 Bataille, *The Accursed Share*, 41.
27 Bataille, *The Accursed Share*, 58–59.
28 Bataille, *The Accursed Share*, 59.
29 Bataille, *The Accursed Share*, 59.
30 Bataille, *The Accursed Share*, 59.
31 Bataille, *The Accursed Share*, 65.
32 Bataille, *The Accursed Share*, 67.
33 Bataille, *The Accursed Share*, 70.
34 Benveniste, 33.
35 Benveniste, 39.
36 Gasché, 103–104.
37 Gasché, 105.
38 Bourdieu, 234–235.
39 Bourdieu, 76–77.
40 Bourdieu, 235.
41 Bourdieu, 236.
42 Bourdieu, 81–91.
43 Bourdieu, 109.
44 Bataille, *The Accursed Share*, 110.
45 Piel, 103.
46 Piel, 103–104.
47 Bataille qtd. in Piel, 104.
48 Piel, 105.
49 Piel, 105.
50 Bataille, *The Accursed Share*, 245.
51 Bataille, *The Accursed Share*, 274.

52 Stoekl, "Bataille, Gift Giving, and the Cold War," 247.
53 Stoekl, "Bataille, Gift Giving, and the Cold War," 248.
54 Stoekl, "Bataille, Gift Giving, and the Cold War," 248.
55 Stoekl, "Bataille, Gift Giving, and the Cold War," 249.
56 Stoekl, "Bataille, Gift Giving, and the Cold War," 249.
57 Stoekl, "Bataille, Gift Giving, and the Cold War," 249.
58 Stoekl, "Bataille, Gift Giving, and the Cold War," 251.
59 Stoekl, "Bataille, Gift Giving, and the Cold War," 251.
60 Stoekl, "Bataille, Gift Giving, and the Cold War," 252.
61 Stoekl, "Bataille, Gift Giving, and the Cold War," 253.
62 Derrida, "Différance," 72.

III
Sovereignty, Transgression, and Power: Bataille's Subject

THE CONCEPTION OF TRANSGRESSION, AS A PRIMARY method of psychological, sexual, and philosophical subversity, acts as the foundation for sovereignty for Bataille. The sovereign subject is a reformed individual; made up of a privileged form of "ascetic experience" with "emotive intellectualism," using philosophers such as Nietzsche or Sade, to create a new, social alterity. Bataille's sovereign subject is, therefore, an "existential figure" who stands "at the end of history" as "incomplete" and a result of Bataille's "tattered humanism."[1]

The influence of Sade is prevalent here, because the libertine's nature also characterizes Nietzsche's Master and/or Overman, and this is the model for Bataille's sovereign man, I argue. The sexual, philosophical, and social combine in Bataille's approach to create a fully transgressive and erotic subject who maintains a presence by way of this radical opposition to the normative order. Bataille's philosophical attraction to Nietzsche's work is evident in both direct and indirect ways; the descriptions he offered of Nietzsche's philosophy as "an incomparable seductive force," as work that mobilized "the will and aggressive instincts" was largely misunderstood in the philosophical tradition, argues Bataille. This occurred because the world that received this work considered it to be "generally unintelligible."[2] This is a cautionary advancement of Nietzsche for Bataille as well, because, as Besnier suggests, "in the political context, the sovereign also incarnates the horror of power which blindly wants the end."[3]

Nietzsche's philosophy advances what Bataille describes as "the transvaluation of values" and "will always belong to all men of action and will."[4] This is more broadly construed in Bataille's two "extremes" of humanity: "civilization and barbarism—or savagery."[5] And further:

> Human life, therefore is composed of two heterogeneous parts which never blend. One part is purposeful [...] The other is primary and sovereign

as either utilitarian and rational or irrational and violent.[6] This leads him to consider Sade from the perspective of something akin to Nietzsche's Will:

> De Sade's expression of violence changes violence into something else, something necessarily its opposite: into a reflecting and rationalized will to violence.[7]

Even Nietzsche's practice of affirmation or "joy before death," is emblematic of a "shameless, indecent saintliness" which "can lead to a sufficiently happy *loss of self*" and this indicates that "life can be gloried from root to summit" for Bataille.[8] Bataille sought to re-establish the importance of Dionysus and tragedy as the model for communal existence out of Nietzsche's work. In "Nietzschean Chronicle" he writes:

> When Nietzsche made DIONYSOS (in other words, the destructive exuberance of life) the symbol of the will to power, he expressed in that way a resolution to deny to a faddish and debilitating romanticism the force that must be held sacred.[9]

This releases humans from a life of "SERVITUDE, IN OTHER WORDS, FROM THE PUNISHMENT OF THE PAST" as well as religious "humility" and the "CONFUSIONS AND TURPOR OF ROMANTICISM" allowing the "BRILLIANT WILL" to return to the Earth.[10] The "headlessness" of this new version of the Will is a community with a headless leader (acephalic man) which is "BOUND TOGETHER BY THE OBESESSIVE IMAGE OF A TRAGEDY" and this is foundationally strengthened by death/sacrifice.[11] This is a "Dionysian truth" which conjoins with Sade's "bloody doctrine," creating a principle of "the law of all or nothing" argues Bataille.[12] For this, Bataille describes how

> Man has escaped from his head just as the condemned man has escaped from his prison [...] He is not a man. He is not a god either. He is not me but is more than me: his stomach is the labyrinth in which he has lost himself, loses me with him, and in which I discover myself as him, in other words as a monster.[13]

The reformation of Nietzsche's philosophy created what Bataille described as a "free human destiny," torn away from "the rational enslavement of production, as well as the irrational enslavement to the past,"[14] leading to the transvaluation of a metaphysical force equal to a sublime experience of the Will; "[t]ransgressing with one's life the laws of reason."[15] This remains fixed in Bataille, as it is in Nietzsche, I would assert, on questions of the "body" or material existence:

> Perhaps the whole evolution of the spirit is just a question of the body. It is the process of development of a higher body looming in our sensibility. The organic is rising to different and higher levels. Our thirst for knowledge of nature is a means through which the body strives to perfect itself.[16]

In "On Nietzsche," the Dionysian figure that underlies Bataille's sovereign philosophy is a subject that exists in "a world delivered from gods, from the concern with salvation," as an "immanent figure" or a "whole man" with a "frivolous life" and Bataille writes the following:

> Essentially, man is only a being in whom transcendence is cancelled, no longer separate from anything: part puppet, part god, part madman.[17]

Dionysus is the best model for the "destructive exuberance of life," a figure who comes from "the realm of dreams and intoxication" and rules the "revel" of the drunken and liberated mob, occupying a space near the limit of death.[18] Bataille's readings of Nietzsche's "sacrificial violence" in the Will's relations of power as a revolt against Christian morality in *Beyond Good and Evil*, ground his interpretation of transgression against religious piety, and where Nietzsche claims "weak beings" are those subservient to Christian theology, Bataille agrees. Nietzsche argues that their fixation with the crucifixion occurs because the "final sacrifice of a god fosters the spiritualization and moralization of human weakness" into "a permanent and dangerous state of perpetual obedience and self-torture," and this permits the communal ideals of sacrifice to be strengthened in Bataille's theory of sovereignty.[19]

Yet, in Bataille's fullest revelation of sovereign revolution and sacrifice, the general disposition of "wholly unproductive sacrifice" which created "metapolitical communities without conventional notions of authority and identity," is not an idea which could be sustained in either a material or social sense, argues Jesse Goldhammer.[20] This is because the sovereign subject remains irreconcilable and "solitary," living in a "tragic fashion" because of the "tortures of negativity without a cause."[21] Bataille's "postwar" (World War II) theories which sought to find "virtue and redemption" via sacrifice and the irreconcilability of excess, only ended in a "repetition of the original crime," and the creation of uselessness, of "violent waste" in refuting inertia and servitude towards sovereignty.[22]

Goldhammer argues that Bataille's "community" never could "repair, restore, or regenerate" anything, as it is "incapable of establishing, founding and inaugurating anything productive" because it "begins" by violating "the limits that make politics possible, and tragically, it must exist in a permanent state of violation."[23] This community is consistently connected to the "event" and appeal of the "sacred, and in its performance" and this enacts a "sacred sociology" rather than a "general or religious sociology" which would be necessary for a functional community.[24] With the *Acéphale* and the *College of Sociology*, there is a "tragic" (Nietzschean) version of the energies "promoted in Contre-Attaque—a form of 'vitalism'" that could ground Bataille's theories of sovereignty and transgression away from art (specific to a period) (Surrealism and poetry) and "into literature" where this "sacred [was] a discourse of action and power."[25] But I think that this problem of communal revolution as a viable form, is doubly shared in regards to Bataille's sovereign subject, as the violation of social and political limits to develop true sovereignty is also what marks the sovereign subject as an *Other* and most fully, *criminal*. Therefore, Sade is the remedy to the problem of the sovereign subject in Bataille.

For Sade, the transgressive subject as criminal is the basis for sovereignty and/or sovereign power, at least in regards to the many anti-establishment acts and philosophical positions of his libertines. Bataille describes Sade as being "Like the sun at least in being intolerable to the naked eye."[26] The libertine is both violent and philosophically "aggressive," in the "casual incoherence" as well as brutal violence which exemplifies his power.[27] And as well, beginning "from an attitude of utter irresponsibility and end[ing] with one of stringent self-control" by way of many crescendos of pleasure, "the peak of sovereignty" is illustrated in Sade for Bataille:

> There is a movement forward of transgression that does not stop before a summit is reached.[28]

This energetic movement, coupled with the indifference towards others (the Libertine credo) "becomes in the end denying oneself."[29] It is not personal "enjoyment" that is of value to the libertine, but more that the "crime is the only thing that counts," and an excess of this is preferred, as it "should reach the pinnacle of crime."[30] This illustrates the end of "inflexible sovereignty" for Bataille, and a "concern for power" in correlation with this transgression makes historical sovereignty a material reality in Bataille's estimation.[31] He describes this as follows: "Real sovereignty is not what it claims to be; it is never more than an effort at freeing human existence from the bonds of necessity," and the sovereign subject is both free because of this (from morality, social norms, and all conventions of humanism) but also a "victim of his own sovereignty."[32] This occurs because he cannot stop, and "the man who denies is the ultimate denial of all else in the universe, a denial which will not even spare him."[33] The "continuity of crime" is like a persistent form of transgressiveness which "transcends nothing" and this "infinite continuity" combines with "infinite destruction," so in the end, there is only ruin: sexual crime and material death.

Nevertheless, for Bataille, it is clear that this reiterates a principle of practical and theoretical "heterology" and crime, transgression, and sovereignty remain, from a heterogeneous perspective, opposed to "any homogeneous representation of the world, in other words, to any philosophical system."[34] "Heterology" serves to reverse the world of order and philosophical clarity (certainty perhaps) and *"now serves excretion; it introduces the demand for violent gratification implied by social life."*[35] The sovereign life is viewed within a range of what Bataille sees as a firm reversal of civilized, social existence, and he writes:

> All organizations that have ecstasy and frenzy as their goal (the spectacular death of animals, partial tortures, orgiastic dances, etc.) will have no reason to disappear when a heterological conception of human life is substituted for the primitive conception.[36]

In their influence, I can see that Nietzsche and Sade permit the sovereign subject in Bataille to possess and enact a *broader* and more or less *ruthless* form of power. In the combination of the Nietzschean Will to Power and the Sadean erotic transgression is the perfect monster of Bataille's sovereign *man*; yet the interiorization of his radical difference provides a different kind of view from either Nietzsche or Sade, as it is a new conscious order. Appropriation and excretion act as conjoined forces that supply energy for this sovereign existence: the excremental and/or collective impulses eventually deflate the "political, juridical, and economic institutions."[37] And further, the power of the taboo and/or heterogeneity creates a "foreign body" which is the manifestation of the "sacred, divine, or marvelous," as a "half-decomposed cadaver" in a profane manifestation, and a product of expenditure out of the liberated excesses of "ambivalence."[38]

The Dionysian revel combines with a Sadean imperative and becomes, for Bataille, the "sacrificial consumption in the elementary form of the orgy to INCORPORATE the person by 'force.'"[39] This is both a rise and a fall, such that first, "Sovereignty is the power to rise, indifferent to death, above the laws which ensure the maintenance of life,"[40] and the sovereign author/philosopher "addresses sovereign humanity, beyond the servitude of the isolated reader."[41] And second, the fall which perpetuates this rise as the "quest for sovereignty by the man alienated by civilization" as the cause of historical agitation (whether it be religious or political, undertaken, according to Marx, because of man's "alienation".)[42]

The "impossible" that is revealed in the moment of "clear consciousness" when sovereignty takes hold, in conjunction with the "movement of free and internally wrenching violence that animates the whole, dissolves into tears, into ecstasy and into bursts of laughter" is "the sovereign self-consciousness" becoming fully constituted.[43] This alienated consciousness is reformed into an "authentic sovereignty," yet Bataille also argues that "one cannot attain it consciously and seek it, because seeking distances it" which reiterates Nietzsche's proclamations regarding the Will.[44]

In the "Schema of Sovereignty," Bataille describes the sovereign "being" as a subject *familiar with death* who "resists individual consciousness, whose principle exists within him," and is therefore not an "animal."[45] This is reinforced in acts of killing, when the sovereign man "escapes the subordination that he refuses," to restore "sovereign existence," although Bataille also remarks that killing is not "the only way to regain sovereign life, but sovereignty is always linked to a denial of the sentiments death controls" as a *violation* of "the prohibition against killing."[46] And as the Will to Power comes to re-create the world and the individual for Nietzsche, so too does the sovereign "world" remove the "limit of death" (in addition to the violence which actualizes death), but the "sovereign is he who *is*, as if death were not" because he transgresses all limits (identity and death) by way of "play" like a "game."[47] I cannot help but think here of the sadistic and brutal "games" of Sade's libertines brought more fully into a philosophical forum. The way that this criminal Other can be rescued from a material history is also fascinating in Bataille's work.

In "The Tragedy of Gilles de Rais," Bataille utilizes the same concepts from sovereignty to examine the crimes of de Rais as an actual historical example, and he describes de Rais as a man of "his time," one of any number of "unreasonable feudal lords, with whom he shares the pleasures of egoism, laziness, and disorder," a person who lived in "contempt of the world."[48] De Rais was a lieutenant who served with Joan of Arc and later, after her execution, a serial killer who preyed on hundreds of children in rural France in the 1400s until he was caught, prosecuted, and executed once he confessed. I would argue that the difficulty with the material existence of a figure composed of Nietzschean Will and Sadean violence is exemplified in the tension in Bataille's treatment of de Rais. Bataille's reiteration of the concept of "play," about de Rais, is not within the scope of what could be described as "childishness" but rather, "*monstrosity*," although this form of monstrousness remains "childlike" for Bataille, it seems an odd application of this theory. He describes de Rais as the following:

> a child as a cannibal is; or more precisely, as one of his Germanic ancestors, unbounded by civilized proprieties.[49]

This allows Bataille to enforce a claim of sovereignty for de Rais, as he becomes what is described as "[j]oined to the god of sovereignty" as a young warrior because of his "bestial ferocity," which is neither limited nor ruled by reason or civility. Added to this is each of de Rais' residences which possessed "a room worthy of the cruel imaginings of Sade, where pleasure was fused to the jerks of dying bodies" of the many children he murdered there.[50] Bataille describes him as a "victim of the profane world, of the real world," who by way of crime, "also possessed a feeling of belonging to the sacred world."[51] He is a sovereign Lord, a "monster before us [who] is like a child," and Bataille writes the following:

> We cannot deny the monstrosity of childhood. How often children would, if they could, be Gilles de Raises![52]

So, like the sovereign man, the Sadean libertine, the Nietzschean Overman, and "the tiger and the child," none are monsters per se, "but in this world where reason rules, their apparent monstrosity is fascinating; they escape the necessary order" as "foolishness and childishness have the habit of escaping attention" argues Bataille.[53] The reality of the sovereign man as a libertine monster, and the idealization of his command of the Will to Power more generally, cannot become actualized in any positive way in the world I assert, as these things are compelled by violence, mastery over others, and power/transgression in its most brutal forms. This creates contradictions between the strong and the weak which can never be supported as metaphysically beneficial or enlightened for sovereign subjects. And as is true of Bataille's descriptions of de Rais, sovereign subjects cannot ever be objects of adoration, as their acts and their very constitution as subjects indicate a deviation from the basic intellectual and individual standards of what is "best" about themselves or others. This tension between advocating de Rais as an example of sovereign strength and power, yet also condemning him for his brutal acts, is what Bataille struggles with, and indeed, is the paradox at the heart of sovereignty, in general, I conclude.

Notes

1   Besnier, 20.
2   Bataille, "Nietzsche and the Fascists," in *Visions of Excess*, 185.
3   Besnier, 2.
4   Bataille, "Nietzsche and the Fascists," in *Visions of Excess*, 187.
5   Bataille, *Erotism*, 186.
6   Bataille, *Erotism*, 193.
7   Bataille, *Erotism*, 191.
8   Bataille, *Visions of Excess*, 237.
9   Bataille, *Visions of Excess*, 206.
10 Bataille, *Visions of Excess*, 207.
11 Bataille, *Visions of Excess*, 210.
12 Bataille, *Visions of Excess*, 210–211.
13 Bataille, *Visions of Excess*, 181.
14 Bataille, *Visions of Excess*, 194.

15 Bataille, *Visions of Excess*, 193.
16 Nietzsche, *Hammer*, 37
17 *The Bataille Reader*, 338.
18 Bataille, *Visions of Excess*, 207.
19 Goldhammer, 16–17.
20 Goldhammer, 190.
21 Besnier, 21.
22 Goldhammer, 190–191.
23 Goldhammer, 191.
24 Guerlac, 208.
25 Guerlac, 208.
26 Bataille, *Erotism*, 179.
27 Bataille, *Erotism*, 192.
28 Bataille, *Erotism*, 175.
29 Bataille, *Erotism*, 175.
30 Bataille, *Erotism*, 175.
31 Bataille, *Erotism*, 174.
32 Bataille, *Erotism*, 174.
33 Bataille, *Erotism*, 176.
34 Bataille, "The Use Value of D. A. F. de Sade," in *Visions of Excess*, 97.
35 Bataille, "The Use Value of D. A. F. de Sade," in *Visions of Excess*, 97.
36 Bataille, "The Use Value of D. A. F. de Sade," in *Visions of Excess*, 102.
37 Bataille, "The Use Value of D. A. F. de Sade," in *Visions of Excess*, 94.
38 Bataille, "The Use Value of D. A. F. de Sade," in *Visions of Excess*, 95.
39 Bataille, "The Use Value of D. A. F. de Sade," in *Visions of Excess*, 95.

40 Bataille, "The Use Value of D. A. F. de Sade," in *Visions of Excess*, 155.
41 Bataille, "The Use Value of D. A. F. de Sade," in *Visions of Excess*, 160.
42 Bataille, *Literature and Evil*, 165.
43 *The Bataille Reader*, 277–278.
44 *The Bataille Reader*, 293.
45 *The Bataille Reader*, 317.
46 *The Bataille Reader*, 318.
47 *The Bataille Reader*, 319.
48 Bataille, *The Trial of Gilles de Rais*, 25.
49 Bataille, *The Trial of Gilles de Rais*, 33.
50 Bataille, *The Trial of Gilles de Rais*, 38.
51 Bataille, *The Trial of Gilles de Rais*, 16.
52 Bataille, *The Trial of Gilles de Rais*, 24.
53 Bataille, *The Trial of Gilles de Rais*, 24.

IV
Transgression, Art, and Surrealism: In-between the Avant-Garde and Literature

In "The Notion of Expenditure," Bataille describes the "principle of loss" as an "unconditional expenditure," and this is best seen in the "bloody wasting of men and animals in *sacrifice*" such that "in the etymological sense of the word, sacrifice is nothing other than the production of sacred things."[1] This illustrates the symbolic expenditures that occur in art, especially any avant-garde movement which opposes the social or rational order, and in moving the "great night,"[2] the avant-garde group or artist creates an aesthetic revolution by way of a "state of excitation" that is "comparable to toxic states" of "illogical and irresistible impulse to reject material or moral goods."[3] The revolutionary fervor of this aesthetics is clear for Bataille.

For Mary Ann Caws, the "outlook and inscape" of Surrealist production, as a primary example I will use here, had a dual function: energy that is dominated by the inscape is a "communication between the two sides of the Surrealists' swinging door," and next, it functions as a "two-way passage" revealed by insight and confronted by oppositional forces. This is a form of liminality; between what is seen and the observer or "what is in and what is out" of the frame.[4] She argues that this "labyrinth," or "packets of labyrinths" is also a form of internalization (spatially understood as in an interior creation), and externalization (as in aesthetic and theoretical dialectical intervention), and therefore, sovereignty and transgression are primary functions of an artistic counter-culture or community.[5]

I will describe a series of artistic and generative forces in the avant-garde activities of Surrealism to place Bataille within a context of aesthetic transgression, and to indicate the *inbetweeness* that he experienced here. But it is essential to recognize the main division between Breton and the Surrealists in the *Second Surrealist Manifesto* where Breton characterizes Bataille as being psychopathological concerning expenditure and nothing else, he describes him as a pathological "case" because, as John Lechte suggests, Breton assumes he "is obsessed with manure and, more generally, with impurity and defilement."[6] "No beauty without defilement, is Bataille's dictum" according to Breton, Lechte argues. Yet, Breton is the same author who found "sudden cataclysms, great popular manifestations of madness, riots, [and] enormous revolutionary slaughters" as the "backlash" of avant-garde or surrealist art.[7] In "The Lugubrious Game," he finds that the "irrevocable ugliness" of Picasso and Dali's paintings is comparable to detestable "beauties":

> the beauty that conceals nothing, the beauty that is not the mask of ruined immodesty, the beauty that never contradicts itself and remains eternally at attention like a coward.[8]

Dali, who refused the use/reproduction of his paintings in Bataille's essay, ends up being the target of his critique of artistic superficiality, and it is Dali's work that exemplifies the "cowardice and the poverty of spirit" of this "game" which allows the Surrealists to retreat and hide in the "'wonderland' of Poetry without being publicly condemned" as cowards, asserts Bataille.[9] For Bataille, the result of this aesthetic assessment is twofold: first, to "nauseate Dali" and second, to cause all viewers to "squeal like a pig before his canvases."[10] Surrealism, he writes, is "a childhood disease" of base materialism; the intellectual and materialist imperatives which enact a series of "pretentious idealistic aberrations" and this originates out of an "unhappy bourgeois" that has

> maintained a human vulgarity, a certain taste for virility, disaffection with his own class [which] quickly turns into stubborn hatred.[11]

This alienated upper class seeks to "create its own values in order to oppose established values" by way of "blinding flashes and disheartening attacks of empty verbiage" in the revision of concepts such as: "*spirit, surreal, absolute.*"[12] The primary discourse of these avant-gardist "bourgeois revolutionaries" creates a "cheap utopian blindness" writes Bataille.[13] This occurs because the unconscious loses its force and becomes "no more than a pitiable treasure trove" for Breton. What is left is a useless "provocation" that is merely a mockery of revolutionary action, argues Bataille.[14] In this way, the Surrealists play "the role of juvenile victims" and produce manifestos such as the *Second Surrealist Manifesto* which exhibits "their obsession with unhealthiness," their obsession with the "poetic," and the passage from "brilliant shadow play to the *failed acts* that today underlie human existence" like a "*degraded* ladder."[15] This "servile idealism" is accompanied by a "peevish aristocracy" and "mental askesis" writes Bataille.[16] And this formula for surrealist dysfunction places the "role of the sun" in a central position, where Breton is Icarus.[17] It is evident that "surrealism can only be pursued as negation," asserts Bataille, without respect for history because of its "moral infantilism to pass to free subversion, the basest subversion."[18]

Despite the obvious dissatisfaction that Bataille felt concerning surrealism, the transgressive nature of the collective or group was still a central idea he supported; it was Breton that proved to be the problem. And with *Acéphale* and the *College of Sociology*, the "tragic (Nietzschean) version of the transgression he foregrounded in his philosophy," remained evidently "connected to poetry and surrealism," yet moved "away from art" by retreating into literature using the sacred and profane as its basis, argues Suzanne Guerlac.[19] The "surrealist revolt" or "scandal" still worked as a provocative and defiant position against social morality and convention, unveiling what was/is

> camouflaged: the so-called shameful parts of the human body, the exploitation of man by man, the existence of torture, but also the too unbearable brilliancy of a person out of step with his environment.[20]

This "subversion" is a correlate to transgression, as it is "a force of resistance and upheaval" which is the "fundamentally poetic element in [the] surrealist endeavor," argues Matthews.[21] But these forces were divisive between Breton and Bataille, and as Lechte describes it, these could be understood by way of an analysis of vertical versus horizontal axes: Surrealism (and Breton) used "psychobiography" and a medicalized framework to view Others "between the normal and the pathological," and referred itself to transcendence via the vertical "objectification, conceptualization, representation" or "*theoria*" argues Lechte.[22] "Horizontality," on the contrary, "refers to immanence, and thus, secondarily, to ritual, difference, horror silence, heterogeneity, abjection," and it is inherently "non-discursive," and this axis typifies Bataille's approach to aesthetics or philosophy/literature.[23]

The main material difference between these is the Surrealist's use of metaphor, and Bataille's reliance on metonymy, and this comes to define the "relationship between Bataille and Surrealism" more generally.[24] Surrealist "poetry begins to erase the gap between word and image" through a "fusion of inner (poetry) and outer (image) poetry and painting unite with one another."[25] Lechte writes: "Painting becomes poetic, and poetry uses painting's image to create '*the image present to the mind*.'"[26] This completes the unity of "dream and reality" by way of metaphor for Breton. Bataille, on the other hand, uses "horror, ecstasy and obscenity" to bring this metaphorical process to "a halt."[27] This terminates any kind of reliance on only image and word, defeating the linguistic and dominant practice of Surrealist painters and poets towards the "other" that it seeks to represent or "objectify."[28] As Lechte describes it:

> In a certain sense, Bataille writes in order to put out the light of the sun. That is, he writes in order to bring metaphor to an end.[29]

He wants to "render language opaque," and to delimit the limitations of representation.[30] He does this by way of utilizing the "metonymy of desire which produces writing" to the extreme of "horror, jouissance and death."[31] This occurs within a "universe of joy—ecstasy—and horror," where the illumination of the sun is both enlightening and blinding, and writing informs, yet is exhausted to death.[32]

The aesthetic production of this transgressive context is a fuller account of what and how art functions, and

Briony Fer's essay concerning painting and Bataille specifies this relation in regards to Bataille's relationship with Miró, Masson, Picasso, and Dali.[33] Bataille allied himself with these artists and their "desire to kill painting by its own means" as a "kind of confession" and from Miró, specifically: "I want to murder painting" (1927).[34] The central tenets of modern painting as "annihilation and obliteration" is connected to violence or subversion, and this appealed to Bataille most heartily.[35] Yet, art cannot serve as a substitute for violence for Bataille, as it is first, an anti-theological movement, and second, a reinforcing of the strange, obscene, and fantastical that belongs to the ritualistic. Finally, in a third way, it acts to support a reinvention of narrative in the literary sphere.

For Bataille, art must proceed "by successive destructions" so it can "liberate" libidinal instincts which are "sadistic" in their nature.[36] Drawing allows him to propose a theory of "prehistory" for art, and this is "where art's unconscious is to be found."[37] Incoherence in a narrative, or a fragmented surface of meaning for a work of art suggests to Bataille that the obliteration of meaning has already occurred, yet the remainder of the work is still present, and this is a "state of absence, of indifference and silence" that "is characteristic of modern painting" more generally, and perhaps modern literature as well.[38] This "trajectory" of transgression highlights those "exemplary moments in the history of art" which combine the "erotic and the sadistic," and in *The Tears of Eros* (1967), even Surrealism is placed by Bataille into this framework. Like the "modern literary text, modern painting rehearses the cruelty of sacrifice on its own means of representation" moving from the cave paintings at Lascaux as a moment of prehistoric conscious/unconscious aesthetic creation, into the modern forms of artistic "destruction of objects 'in a field of attraction induced by a flashing point (*pointe*) where solid forms are destroyed'" then "consumed as in a blazing mass (*brasier*) of light."[39] Sacrifice, mutilation, dismemberment, violence, and castration are the emblems of Bataille's transgressive aesthetics, and the key figures for this remain Sade and Freud's "uncanny" (*unheimlich*) or "the something secretly familiar but buried" like the "destructive femininity of Pandora's box."[40]

The key term and/or concept from Bataille's philosophy, that Suzanne Guerlac argues is integral to poststructuralism and on into postmodernism, is "transgression," and as an inheritance from Bataille, the contradiction between Surrealism and transgression placed Bataille "not only at the cultural margins during the 1930s but, he was at the edge of these margins" as well.[41] This created a "relation of contestation" which could be seen at its fullest in his difficult correspondence with André Breton and the Surrealists. Guerlac writes: "If Breton was the avant-gardist, Bataille was the ultra- (and perhaps anti-) avant-gardist."[42] Transgression and this "anti" positioning of himself and his work allowed Bataille to build a kind of momentum for poststructuralists to follow, such as Foucault, Phillipe Sollers, and groups like Tel Quel, and further still with Derrida and the postmodern. Transgression was/is a "quasi-philosophical term," but also a "transgression of philosophy" itself, and this created a number of aesthetic subcategories and events in terms of literature and art.[43]

For Bataille, transgression was "a kind of supplement to philosophical discourse," yet the one "isolated" gesture from his work that had the "greatest impact for avant-garde thinking" in the 1960s and 1970s was undoubtedly his use of "an ethnological distinction [of the] sacred/profane into the discourse of philosophy," argues Guerlac.[44] The aesthetic and/or artistic possibilities of the sacred and profane are essential to understanding Bataille's approach to radicalism in art, and the "sacred" appears as "something forbidden" or "impossible," as "there is, as in dreams, an endless contradiction that multiplies without destroying anything" in opposition to the profane which is the domain of the excessive and destructive.[45] Like Nietzsche's Apollonian dream as it is correlated to the Dionysian revel, the interdependence between these two energies are what creates the radicalized moment of artistic creation/intention.

Michel Foucault's "A Preface to Transgression," proposes that transgression might be understood as an equivalent of profanation in a world that no longer "gives any positive meaning to the sacred."[46] And this is also Bataille's central thesis in *Absence of Myth* where transgression is therefore a *psycho-social relief* or a *refusal* of this cathartic release because it reinforces sexual/erotic outcomes. For Foucault, the strong influences of Sade and Nietzsche in Bataille's work created two distinct energies that remained explicit and foundational; especially in his literature. Foucault found that Bataille's transgression is a "gesture which concerns the limit," like a "flash of lightning," or a "figure of the line."[47] But it is also a "play" upon this line or limit, and as Guerlac remarks, transgression is known by way of "two gestures, which are ambiguously one: the inscription of a line and its crossing."[48] Foucault's conclusion finds that it is "the affirmation of difference" which creates a "philosophy of eroticism" as both an inquiry and a reformation: as a "question of language—and the language of philosophy" at its very heart.[49] Where Foucault admits that this is a "crucial reversal" because "if transgression constitutes a philosophy, what is transgressed is the position of the philosopher," it is also true that the work of transgressive philosophy cannot be anything but aesthetically and radically different.[50]

Transgression as a possible form of a revolutionary aesthetic was also accompanied by an idea of "mechanistic calculation of means and ends" after World War II for Bataille, argues Guerlac, and he came to believe that writing must now be based in "freedom" and this transgression of form and limit was best captured in literature.[51] "Against Breton, he opposed a *vitalist* notion of action to literary estheticism," and "[a]gainst Sartre, he opposed a *vitalist* conception of poetry to an instrumental notion of action."[52] This vitalism is problematic, nonetheless, as it contains both its strength (in energy) and demise (in exhaustion of this energy). In Bataille's literature,

> the void, the erotic, excrement and the sources of all kinds of horror, coming from the exorbitant outside, put the subject in question to the point of death

and therefore, "writing" and literature itself are "impossible, dogged by blindness."[53] In *Story of The Eye, Madame Edwarda, The Blue of Noon*, and *The Impossible*, the horizontal and heterogeneous function as "expenditure without return," and as a "will to write" which is either terrifying or sublime, and it continues to offer the reader an insight as well as "blindness," in its operation. This reinforces Lechte's description of Bataille's literature as an aesthetics of "abjection," or what I will next argue is a form of "Outsider" literature.[54]

Notes

1 Bataille, *Visions of Excess*, 119.
2 Bataille, *Visions of Excess*, 121.
3 Bataille, *Visions of Excess*, 128.
4 Caws, 89.
5 Caws, 95–96.
6 Lechte, 118.
7 Bataille, *Visions of Excess*, 27.
8 Bataille, *Visions of Excess*, 27.
9 Bataille, *Visions of Excess*, 29.
10 Bataille, *Visions of Excess*, 28.
11 Bataille, "The 'Old Mole,'" in *Visions of Excess*, 32.
12 Bataille, "The 'Old Mole,'" in *Visions of Excess*, 33.
13 Bataille, "The 'Old Mole,'" in *Visions of Excess*, 34.
14 Bataille, "The 'Old Mole,'" in *Visions of Excess*, 39.
15 Bataille, "The 'Old Mole,'" in *Visions of Excess*, 40–41.
16 Bataille, "The 'Old Mole,'" in *Visions of Excess*, 41.
17 Bataille, "The 'Old Mole,'" in *Visions of Excess*, 42.

18 Bataille, "The 'Old Mole,'" in *Visions of Excess*, 43.
19 Guerlac, 208.
20 Mitrani qtd. in Matthews, 131–132.
21 Matthews, 134.
22 Lechte, 119–120.
23 Lechte, 120.
24 Lechte, 121.
25 Lechte, 121–122.
26 Breton, qtd. in Lechte, 122.
27 Lechte, 122.
28 Lechte, 124.
29 Lechte, 124.
30 Lechte, 125–126.
31 Lechte, 126.
32 Lechte, 126–127.
33 Fer, 155.
34 Fer, 155.
35 Fer, 157.
36 Bataille qtd. in Fer, 157.
37 Fer, 157.
38 Fer, 158.
39 Bataille qtd. in Fer, 159.
40 Fer, 169.
41 Guerlac, 12.
42 Guerlac, 12.
43 Guerlac, 13.
44 Guerlac, 14.
45 Bataille, "The Schema of Sovereignty," in *Visions of Excess*, 314.
46 qtd. in Guerlac, 14.
47 qtd. in Guerlac, 14.

48 Guerlac, 14.
49 Guerlac, 15.
50 qtd. in Guerlac, 16.
51 Guerlac, 209.
52 Guerlac, 209.
53 Lechte, 128–129.
54 Lechte, 129.

V
Outsider Literature(s) inside the Abyss

It would be impossible to write about Bataille's work and his relevance to modern philosophy without a full consideration of the central role of his literary work. In these texts, the narrator or set of narratives that are abject or Other to themselves, and as a literature that composes transgression into material representation, Bataille's literary works never fail to engage and enact a set of principles that originate out of his philosophical theories. The reinvention of language and narrative he brought about, was effectively transmitted by cruelty and displacement, where text and meaning ruptured, and further, the creative potential for violence occurred routinely and randomly. This is founded on a kind of ambivalent yet affirmative affectation for Bataille, something like "the brilliance and suffocation" he described for Sade's work, as "excretion and APPROPRIATION" or a dynamic, heterological system.[1] The "science of heterogeneity" is comprised of limitation versus "violently alternating antagonism (expulsion) and love (reabsorption),"[2] so one sees the "specific character of fecal matter," of ghosts, and as well, "unlimited time or space."[3]

This is always an "anti-social" aesthetic and literature, as it originates from impulses that oppose the interests of "a society in a state of stagnation."[4] The sadist/philosopher/author exists in a world ruled by the "solar anus," argues Bataille, whose "two primary motions are rotation and sexual movement."[5] And this is a universe where

> a dog [is] devouring the stomach of a goose, a drunken vomiting woman, a sobbing accountant [and] a jar of mustard represents the confusion that serves as a vehicle of love.[6]

"Beings [that] only die to be born, in the manner of phalluses that leave bodies in order to enter them," populate this environment.[7] After the death of God, Bataille, like Nietzsche, finds that the birth of the "man-god" who "appears and dies both as rottenness and as redemption of the supreme person" creates "ME."[8] This is an "ideally brilliant and empty infinity" ruled by "catastrophe"[9] and this is the horizon that characterizes his fictional works.

The split subject of literature, and those narrators and characters who come to inhabit the universe(s) of his novels, show the tension between the "monocephalic society" and the "bi- or poly-cephalic society," where the latter serves as the model for a rejection of democratic enslavement in the mono culture or society.[10] This bi- or poly-cephalic existence is governed by "ecstatic time," where visions of things like "cadavers, nudity, explosions, spilled blood, abysses, sunbursts, and thunder," are the signs and symptoms of an *unfinished* kind of existence, or of a "world like a bleeding wound" for Bataille.[11] *Bi/auto/biography* is the form this adopts, I argue, as a split graphism and aesthetic approach to literature for Bataille: both a chronicle of the external acts and events in his own life, but also a kind of universal narrative that unveils the darker aspects of his (and everyone else's) development into Otherness. He describes the process of this form of writing as follows:

> And at the same time it is necessary to strip away all eternal representations from what is there, until it is nothing but a pure violence, an interiority, a pure inner fall into a limitless abyss; this point endlessly absorbing from the cataract all its inner nothingness, in other words, all that has disappeared, is "past," and in that same movement endlessly prostituting a sudden apparition to the love that vainly wants to grasp that which will cease to be.[12]

This recognition of impending and/or actual loss creates the desire in the transgressive subject for writing, and this writing, therefore, originates out of an abject moment of conscious anxiety: "Nothing is more desirable than what will soon disappear."[13]

I would have you consider how Kristeva's idea of abjection could serve as the foundation for understanding this anxiety as the

> experience that is always a contradiction between the presence of a subject and its loss, between thought and its expenditure which eroticism fuels.[14]

It is clear that it works in two ways towards this erasure of the subject and its severance from the world, and then, the creation of "a contradiction of it." The body, as a central concern in Bataille's literature, is treated in this way; bodies and more particularly women's bodies are routinely structured or depicted as two-way hallways or corridors/rooms, like labyrinths, ruined cathedrals, and gigantic icons/monuments that seem "determined to disappear" as they come to form the landmarks for the "urge for death or disappearance within the passes of the erotic."[15] His novels are "orgasmic texts" argues Smith, which conjure up depictions of more general concepts of "the interior body," and in texts like *My Mother*, *Madame Edwarda*, *Story of the Eye*, and "Filthy," there is reiteration of the same forms (bodies) which allow for dual representation. Women are sacred yet profane, interior and exterior, known and unknown to the narrator and others (as well as themselves), and finally, they are the tools of literary design that are extinguishable and extinguished. This is done within the privacy and limits of the text and narrative, as well as outside of these boundaries.

This works like an inside/outside and downward/upward series of movements in Bataille's books: there is a downward movement, like one you would experience coming down a circular staircase, and in Bataille's specular construction of Simone in *Histoire de L'oeil* (*Story of the Eye*) when the narrator moves from a description of her face to her genitals as ("sa chair rose et noir"). This is opposite to the upward movement in Baudelaire's poem about Lola de Valance, when he moves from the jewel that is her genitals up to her face, as one would ascend the staircase.[16] These two movements fluctuate in many parts of *Story of the Eye*, yet the downward spiral seems to be the predominant structure, and in this, all characters and events move downward to death or "the end" of the narrative. As Suleiman suggests, *Story* is a "book about the very processes that nourish the pornographic imagination," yet "it is no accident that in *Historie de L'oeil* the narrative of sexual excesses is only 1 part of the work," while the second

> consists of a commentary that traces the fantasmatic elaboration of the obscene narrative from a number of events and people in the narrator's life.[17]

This pornographic "reading" of Bataille's *Story of the Eye* is an avant-garde or modern reconstruction of a classical, literary interpretation, argues Suleiman, and it is presented as a "dialectic of outrage" which qualifies

Bataille's text as "repulsive, obscure, inaccessible; in short to what is, or seems to be, not wanted."[18] Suleiman suggests that because Bataille's deconstruction of the Body and narrative (and bodies more generally), appears as a "glissement" or "sliding" in language, like an architectural form of literature combined with philosophy, his *work*

> provided metaphoric equivalents for his key concepts, as well as a locus for their elaboration: the eroticized female body.[19]

This is a "new architexte" or a pornography of "death," where a "spatial principle of organization" is developed or made material.[20] It consists in "the obscene playing with or defiling" of certain "objects [...] that are essential to high-class pornography: eggs, eyes, hard-boiled, soft-bodied."[21] As well, this is a literature that mounts a "negative attack on Christian ideology and art," as a "thetic moment of process" which utilizes representations of "merely detached substances, isolated from the process of fragmentation."[22] The "literary adventure" for Bataille, as Kristeva suggests, is a "new practice": the moment of negativity and fetishism, the abandonment of the idea of community in regards to these, and the problem of the "closed" nature of the Subject/Self.

> He rehabilitates the tangible and human activity of the *self* but only in order to denounce the illusions it fosters. He insists upon the unity of the human spirit, but in order to rediscover the sacrifice therein and the self—for death.

He proclaims love and fusion, but for their relatedness to death.[23]

This *doubleness* characterizes Bataille's literature (and philosophy) and ensures it is doubly charged: sovereignty and sacrifice, the earth and/or relation between Self/Other, act/reaction, world/text, and as the general and restricted economies of human history and consciousness are all operative as dual phenomena. Suleiman suggests that Bataille's transgression is indivisible from the consciousness of the constraint or prohibition that it violates, and this reinforces the idea of a double entendré, so

> the characteristic feeling accompanying transgression [...] is one of intense pleasure (at the exceeding of boundaries) *and* of intense anguish (at the full realization of the force of those boundaries).[24]

Eroticism *produces* the combination of pleasure and anguish in an "acute" way, and this, in conjunction with the practice of "sexual perversions," reinforces a *glissement* in the writing of the text, as well as the fullest manifestation of "transgressive experience," where the self becomes "unstable, [and/or] 'sliding,'" as well.[25] The doubled subject of the text and in addition, the subject who reads the text, is an unstable formation that Leslie Hill argues is also evident in Nietzsche and Sade's literature: they "deny the reader any stable place that would allow him or her any self-identify *as* a reader" by *inventing* a relationship with history, tradition, language, and being in this double sense.[26] In these invented spaces, time is suspended, and a literary/philosophical vacuum is created, so the "legacy" of transgression, doubleness, suspension, and "silence" continues, and "language divides against itself."[27] In this moment of writing/text, language

> becomes perpetually and irreducibly double: it affirms the need for discourse, but it also bears witness to that which, within words themselves, remains unspoken unspeakable, absolutely other.[28]

Bataille's awareness of this phenomenon can be seen in his declaration of being both "Saint and buffoon," and his "situation" is doubly affected by what he refers to as an "échéance."[29] This exists both as a "chance encounter or event" which is aimed at the individual alone, as well as "a debt, one that falls due on a given date" as in death.[30] This is why "it is necessary to write" states Bataille, yet to also pose the question: "But how to write?" especially when literature "is simply not present wherever philosophy takes it to be."[31] This "incompatibility between literature and philosophy" is perhaps a matter of serious inquiry or rigor, but only "because philosophy and literature relate differently to what lies on their borders" argues Hill.[32] Where "philosophy secures it borders" and regulates its inquiry and objects under consideration,

> literature plainly does not know what is good
> for it; it is irresponsible, lacks seriousness,
> purpose, or proper methodology.[33]

This relationship is an interdependent and antagonistic one, as literature exerts a radical influence upon philosophy,

> for all language without discrimination, including that used by philosophy, bears within it the potential to become literature.[34]

In Bataille's novels/poetry, "literature intervenes within philosophical discourse as an unavoidable, irreducible supplement, the effect of which is to interrupt the clarity and distinctness of philosophical reflection and give voice to the unmasterable turbulence at the heart" of this kind of writing.[35]

Bataille's novels allow the [hu]man to become "erotic animal and religious animal as well," so the "positive result of the dialectic of erotic sovereignty" is invented in literature.[36] "We approach the void," writes Bataille,

> but not to fall into it. We want to become intoxicated with dizziness and the *image* of the fall is enough.[37]

Bataille's fiction is "a desired or intentional fiction" which suggests death and/or the experience of the limit, rather than enforcing it literally.[38] Transgression remains "a function of bodies, determinate bodies that can enter into a dialectical relation" if only as a "sense of fiction" on Bataille's part, argues Guerlac; only with "meanings [...] and with lucidity."[39] Therefore, for Bataille, fiction is "necessary to enable consciousness of the erotic moment" and as is true of sacrifice, this "requires a fictive negation."[40] Together, fiction and negation produce an excitement that is *sensual and/or horrible*, I would add.

The positioning and the presence of women in his literary texts are difficult, as woman is the "erotic object" that renders eroticism "perceptible" to (male) consciousness via "animal sexuality," but this involves a "loss or expenditure" as Woman is the "paradoxical object" or "an object that signifies the absence of any object": beautiful, prostitute, mother, lover, and psychopath, often simultaneously.[41] "Beauty," for Bataille, is always unveiled in nakedness, as a "revelation of beauty which reveals the 'individual charm' of a woman," but this is also a veil that "seduces the man into desiring the woman's non-beautiful parts" or those things that belong more properly to the animal.[42] Bataille writes in *Erotism*: "The beauty of the desirable woman suggests her private parts the hairy ones, to be precise, the animal ones" are negated by such beauty and both the awakening and the exasperation of desire come about through the "exalting [of] her animal parts" alone.[43]

The reader, male narrator, or spectator of these fictional women cooperates with the specular knowledge of the women held there. This is akin to a play on Dionysus with Dianus who Bataille describes as both a "bearded woman and that of a god who is dying, his throat streaming with blood."[44] This *double bind* for the women being narrated, the narrator, and finally, the reader becomes *amplified* in regards to the interruptions or dislocations which create gaps in the fiction, and this textual economy is one that can be read, again, as a struggle between philosophy and literature. In *The Blue Of Noon*, *Story of The Eye*, *Madame Edwarda*, *My Mother*, and *Divine Filth*, Bataille's writing is "the site of a twofold movement" as an "articulation and withdrawal, inscription and effacement," creating an "oscillation" between the "discursive and the fictional, the public and the private, the philosophical and the confessional," argues Leslie Hill.[45]

Bataille described this, in part, as a "double source of choice" where "abuse [and] exploitation" is what breaks "communication" and sacrifice is "what reestablishes it."[46] In poetry, the "most profound importance" is

> the sacrifice of words, of images, and by virtue of the misery of this sacrifice [...] it causes a slipping from impotent sacrifice of objects to that of the subject themselves.

For Bataille, this is best seen in Rimbaud who sacrificed not only poetry as an object, but the poet as subject: "detestable survival but much more upsetting than death the author put to death by his work," is what characterizes his radicalism, he asserted.[47] The author either outlives or is killed by his or her text, and for Bataille, the nuances of subtle changes in his own life recorded such death in different ways. Hill describes "five times over, in 1928, 1935, 1941, 1943 and 1959, Bataille's writing underwent an important sideways shift into literary fiction," and these times correspond to "a moment of intense personal (and political) crisis" in Bataille's life. These moments remained private for Bataille, mainly because his fiction depicted "his own personal life" in "oblique ways," and often, his literary works were suspended or only reservedly circulated or published.[48] For example, *The Blue of Noon* was circulated among a small group of his friends, initially, and both *Story of the Eye* and *Madame Edwarda* were published under pseudonyms in "limited numbers." As a result, the "fictional economy of Bataille's work" remains a "space of singularity" argues Hill, mainly because these texts don't literally "speak to the exchange economy of the author's name."[49] *L'Abbé C* in 1950 and *The Blue of Noon* (1957) are the only two exceptions in this anonymous or oblique authorial economy because they both transformed his "proper" name and signature into "something akin to an assumed name" as well.[50]

For Hill, this leads to a consideration of the author's "death" or rather, "non-existence" as an integral component in Bataille's "literature," and this as a doubled kind of interruption. First, Bataille's literature interrupted philosophical discourse as a "necessary hiatus" from philosophy in his own work/life, and second, his literary work "interrupts its own commitment to narrative continuity" and this is seen on the level of the text itself.[51] Bataille's stories (narratives) are often "elliptical, inconclusive, or fragmentary," and rarely "do they achieve closure" or introduce clear "beginnings" of any kind. His content is "heterogeneous, [like] an improper space," and the effect is both "thematic" and "textual" in regards to this material content. Further, Bataille used pieces from other writers' works, both literally and informally, so fiction was "always already parodic" because of literature's "persistent movement of duplication and replication" of its own difference.[52]

These "pieces" compose a pastiche and "operate like so many *possible* frames of reading," and because of this, they are "elusive," and no single frame "embraces the text as a whole."[53] These defer and/or prevent any direct or singular interpretation of the text by the reader, but they also allow for "different possibilities of reading" argues Hill.[54] Therefore, "reading," like "writing" for Bataille, is "a battle in which no circumstance is without ambiguity."[55] Hill asks:

> In the antagonistic encounter staged by Bataille between philosophy and literature, which has the prior claim? What comes first, fiction or theory? Is the one capable of outdoing the other? Can writing which is without name respond to the challenge of thinking further than either philosophy or literature?[56]

This is a relationship between philosophy and truth, where literature cannot "speak limitlessness or excess any more than philosophy can," so Bataille's literature does not or cannot literally transgress thought because, first, "transgression has always already occurred as a condition of the limit itself" (the text), and second, "because whatever is beyond the limit is by that token *beyond* language."[57] The most important thing in this relationship for Bataille was

> the effort and decision of literature to expose itself to the impossibility of its own foundation [...] as both possibility and impossibility.[58]

If philosophy's judgment upon literature is that it "is always illegitimate and inadequate," then Bataille's literary *response* is formulated by way of a "dual process of inscription and erasure" in first-person narratives which use self-conscious forms of address that enable the work/text to *contain* yet reveal "a deep secret that cannot be spoken."[59] This is the core of "inner experience," one that takes on a literary form for Bataille, where the question of experience has an answer that "vanishes" "in a profound silence."[60] This experience "no longer exists anywhere but in the hidden recesses of the heart."[61] The author, he writes, is "blind" to the answer or to "perfection," and this is because of his/her own "non-knowledge" where "the mind enters deeper into the lost depths of darkness" because of a "rupture" from this "state of blindness."[62] This is an impossible experience, as well as an intellectual space or place (gap) where Bataille seeks to take his reader. He describes this in *Inner Experience* as follows:

> I don't write for one who would be unable to browse, but for one who, entering into this book, would fall as into a hole.[63]

This makes writing a "seamy enterprise" where his work could "cry out when a reader touches me with a greasy paw."[64] He is saved from the absolute *horror* of such an event by the distance that results from the author *releasing it.*⁶⁵ Yet following this release, the author is again left to face the "abyss" or "void." So what is it that remains for the author? Bataille suggests it is both "laughter" and "anguish," where "anguish," "like laughter," seeks to break "down barriers of isolation" in the same way that

> where breath is suspended [...] human existence reaches the decisive moment of its abandonment and its rupture in the darkness of the universe.⁶⁶

Anguish allows for the "communication of anguish" by way of the "common threat of death" that "weighs upon all humans."⁶⁷ This communication, when it occurs in a world without mythic or sacrificial expenditure, can only be found in literature for Bataille. "The one who writes with his blood" needs to be read, but he also says:

> One mustn't read me: I don't want to be covered with evasions. I propose a challenge, not a book. I offer nothing for insomnia.⁶⁸

Bataille's literature evokes a kind of "hatred for salvation" and is best seen in his proclamation echoing something out of Artaud: "NO LONGER TO WANT TO BE EVERYTHING."⁶⁹ A man can "read," to the "extent that it is sovereign—authentic—literature" which "prolongs in him the haunting magic of performances, tragic or comic," Bataille claims, but this is only a diversion into narrative, more properly.⁷⁰ In "Un-Knowing and Its Consequences," he suggests that using a literary language means that the individual routinely says more "than need strictly be said," because only

> silence can express what one has to say, in a language therefore of disquiet, and in a state of perfect despair.[71]

This sacrifice of linguistic meaning for abject knowledge is better seen in the conversion of ideas into non-language and the "residue" which cannot be part of an established episteme, but is more like the debris of such orders which allows for authentic understanding. This sacrifice, like the animal sacrifice he describes as destroying both "notions" of "life" is based on "the rather frequent desire for horror" that compels such sacrifice. This is also an acknowledgement of the limits of knowledge, as well as an embracing of the unknown and "un-knowing" in the face of death, the sacred, and the world (as profane).[72] To read Bataille's literature, therefore, is to respond to what Hill identifies as "laughing absolutely, by ironizing irony, by sacrificing sacrifice" and in doing this, the reader/author/characters can suspend "the oppressive power of discourse" by way of realizing, simultaneously, the presence of an "extreme power of thought" in conjunction with "its radical impotence."[73] It appears that this integrates sovereignty, sacrifice, and unknowingness into a "schema" for aesthetic expression and reception, so the literary moment/work are pure expressions of *un-knowing*. Bataille offers an astute, yet depressing confession in regards to this:

> I am myself in a world which I recognize as deeply inaccessible to me, since in all relations I have sought to establish with it, there remains something I cannot conquer, so that I remain in a kind of despair.[74]

Violence and transgression work to create/sustain Bataille's narratives by way of creating and sustaining his characters and their essential natures and actions, and this fuels the primary force or energy of these narratives/subjects. Sacrifice and shock work at the limits of these structures as responses in terms of literary affectation, and these operate as both public and private variations of violence. For Bataille, the object of a public secret is: "violence," and "taboos appeared in response to the necessity of banishing violence from the course of everyday life" in correlation with the repression of taboos which "exclude violence from social reality" as those concerning "death" and those concerning "sexuality."[75]

These two exclusions combine into one form of violence, which is the actualization of what is a "profound loathing of noisome, decomposing, sticky, intimate life."[76] This violence presents itself as an individual or subjective "project," and more particularly, art, as it can act as a substitute for actual cathartic relief by way of material or physical violence. For Bataille, interiority/abject subjectivity under such conditions creates a "discontinuity" which characterizes the modern subject, as her "perception that intimate life has been excluded from the movements and operations of a life subordinated to the authority of prohibition."[77] This discontinuity also acquires the force of abjection and the pairing of these two results from a recognition of taboos that are internalized by the subject (which seek to repress or prohibit desires or activities), and their compulsion to remove the abject individual "from the scene of violence." This structure can no longer hold its enforced limit and therefore, the subject/their subjectivity becomes *fascinated yet horrified* by these desires, acts, and representations of violence. The usual, normative sense of "shock and shame" ceases to hold back these desires in the individual and therefore, there is no inhibition of the possibility for violence. This "discontinuous being" argues Apple Igrek, only appears to live "in accordance with social regulation as determined by the banishment of violence," yet "sees itself as participating in the excess of life destroying itself in dazzling, tumultuous upheavals" so that

> discontinuity, translated as interiority in the realm of things (outside *is* inside), takes on the meaning of disguising its innermost truth qua violence.[78]

In the theory of "psychotic realism," the boundaries of ego/not ego or self/Others become mad, or near madness, and there is a psychotic "fascination with the outside world," as well as a desire for total incorporation of certain aspects of this world into one's own consciousness/body.[79] This literal translation of the world onto the body/text becomes a "cosmic," erotic, and aesthetic experience, and this qualifies a "contemporary artistic sensibility" in much of the same way that Bataille himself would have described it.[80] All forms of mediation between the work and the viewer/author are exploded phenomenologically, and art, reality, and the individual are conflated, exaggerated, and brutally interconnected by way of a subjectivity that is "disintegrated into radical exteriority."[81] Both abjection and "disgust" figure as key elements of this realism, as both constitute "negative pleasure," as well as an awareness of the "sublime" which originates from a fascination with the "grotesque" for Swearingen and Cutting-Gray in *Extreme Beauty: Aesthetics, Politics, Death*.[82]

As is true of Bataille's literary endeavors, the nature of the art produced under the influence of psychotic realism cannot be purified of the evil, brutal, and/or obscene nature of its material contents, and therefore, it remains "disgusting," and able to produce "disgust" in the reader or viewer. This disgust is compelled by fascination and at its core, "pleasure" and good/evil, beauty/ugliness, and good/bad are overturned for the subject.[83] Even the author, who may be routinely disgusted with the internal, constituent parts of the obscene, those things which repulse the ego: "urine, blood, sperm, excrement," finds these to be the objects of sexual catharsis: "the overflow enhances the identity of the subject, because it implies existence," but also, it is the psychotic compulsion towards fetishizing, exploring, and representing these collapses between body and world that come to compose the suffering and power of sublimity and anguish in works such as Bataille's.[84]

This "extreme" form of aesthetic function/composition is always present in his literary texts by way of their characters and narrators. In "The Dead Man," Bataille describes Marie's smile as "sawed" onto her face, and this dissociative state begins with the death of her husband Edouard when "an emptiness opened inside her, and bore her upward like an angel," like her bare breasts revealed in a church, the "feeling of the irreparable was draining her."[85] Pierre, the narrator, in *My Mother*, is similarly opened out into the world, saying

> From the first I had sensed that inward upheaval, involuntary and burning, which had made me despair when my half-naked mother had flung herself into my arms.

This became an interweaving of "joy and terror" that "strangled" Pierre from within.[86] His mother, in recounting her youthful experiences, is equally and sublimely affected by the world in states of delirium:

> I preferred being alone, I was alone in the woods, I was naked in the woods, I was naked,

she says,

> I was in a state [...] I shall die without ever recapturing the state I was in, I had forebodings, dreamt of girls or of fauns [...] I would twist on the horse, writhe, I was monstrous and—.[87]

Pierre describes this anguish and sublimity as follows:

> I had a sensation of waters on the rise: the waters were those horrors, and soon there would be no further refuge to take before their mounting: as the drowning man's throat opens to the enormity of the waters, I would succumb to the power of malediction, to the power of woe.[88]

These descriptions reiterate the affectation of a radical exteriority and transgression, and again, in *Madame Edwarda*, the narrator observes a polyphony of visual and experiential sensations and events which become internalized into this fractured subject/character:

> the mirrors wherewith the room's walls were everywhere sheathed and the ceiling too, cast multiple reflections on an animal coupling, but, at each least movement, our bursting heavens would strain wide-open to welcome "the emptiness of heaven."[89]

The excess of expenditure for Edwarda is described as a form of jouissance, of excessive orgasmic energy:

> Edwarda's pleasure—fountain of boiling water, heartbursting furious tideflow—went on and on, weirdly, unendlingly; the stream of luxury, its strident inflexion, glorified her being unceasingly, made her nakedness unceasingly more naked, her lewdness ever more intimate.[90]

In *Story of The Eye*, the narrator/author describes his ecstasy as a kind of synaesthetic connection he finds with the universe through transgression and nausea:

> I stretched out in the grass, my skull on a large, flat rock and my eyes staring straight up at the milky way, that strange breach of astral sperm and heavenly urine across the cranial vault formed by the ring of constellations: that open crack at the summit of the sky

like "a broken egg, a broken eye, or my own dazzled skull weighing down the rock."[91] The obvious presence of the sublime in conjunction with the lewdness of material existence forms a pattern for the subjects held within the pages of Bataille's texts. The narrator describes this as an aesthetic practice:

> My kind of debauchery soils not only my body and my thoughts, but also anything I may conceive in its course, that is to say, the vast starry universe, which merely serves as a backdrop.[92]

The narrator's love life with Simone begins when they happen upon the corpse of an "apparently very young and very pretty girl" whose "head was almost totally ripped off" and they become "fully absorbed in the sight of the corpse."[93] The narrator also observes the following:

> The horror and despair at so much bloody flesh, nauseating in part, and in part very beautiful, was fairly equivalent to our usual impression upon seeing one another.[94]

This "equivalency" he next describes is

> suggestive of all things linked to deep sexuality, such as blood, suffocation, sudden terror, crime; things indefinitely destroying human bliss and honesty,

and this reaches its conclusion when he witnesses Simone's "mute and absolute spasm."[95] This is described by way of the "sun's radiance" that "sucks" Simone and the narrator "into an unreality that fitted our malaise—the wordless and powerless desire to explode and kick up our asses," a "morose dissolution that leaves no harmony between the various spasms of the body."[96] This also becomes an orgiastic event when Marcelle is added to their "brutal frenzy" like a "writhing out of a monster's grip" which was nothing more than the "utter violence of my movements" he says.[97] Women's genitalia/their desire are described in a similar fashion like the "eruptions of volcanoes" which "never turn active except, like storms or volcanoes, with something of catastrophe or disaster."[98] But these spaces are also secretive and dark areas of transgression, as Simone's vagina contains "the wan blue eye of Marcelle," which gazes at the narrator "through tears of urine."[99] It is Simone who is earlier described as something like Deleuze and Guattari's becoming-animal (*A Thousand Plateaus*), who Marcelle "mistook"

> for a wolf because of her black hair, her silence, and because Simone's head was docilely rubbing Marcelle's thigh, like a dog nuzzling his master's leg.[100]

In "Filthy" and "Divinity" (*Divine Filth*), both short stories gravitate around two different forms of Woman-As-Other for Bataille's male narrators: Divinity is "the image of bad luck"[101] and Filthy surveys the narrator with "the eyes of a beast, with "long, grubby hands," and is both "drunk and beautiful," vile and mesmerizing.[102] As a kind of metaphysical statement regarding these excesses, the narrator in "Divinity" says "We were being forced to bear an absence of outlets for excess disgust to issue from us."[103] To the point of misidentification and material transformation, the sublime works at all aspects of the characters in Bataille's novels, and particularly in *Story*, the young characters are most affected by the radical reconfiguration of themselves. Like the reader of this text, there is a "situated" or specific kind of context and positioning of characters, and as Mikhal Popowski argues in "On the Eye of Legibility-Illegibility," there is a "reader's expectation" which is determined by her or his "knowledge and experience," and this is based on a set of preconditions that is usurped by illegibility, leaving the end result as a "failed expectation for the reader" (and characters/narrator as well, I would add).[104] The mark of illegibility guides the fragmented and antagonistic surface of this text, but the important thing for Popowski is that "the reader can be compensated for the lack in his knowledge only if he accepts to play the game of the text and consequently to read it and un-read it [...] in a simultaneous movement."[105] The presentation and practice of illegibility/legibility is "an integral part of the textual thematics, an integral part of its discourse, an integral part of the text itself," and this absolutely reflects Bataille's broader philosophical and aesthetic work.[106] Bataille argues that there "exists no prohibition that cannot be transgressed" and his literature, as an enacting of this imperative, consistently seeks to prove that this is true.[107]

Notes

1 Bataille, "The Use Value of D. A. F. de Sade," in *Visions of Excess*, 93.
2 Bataille, "The Use Value of D. A. F. de Sade," in *Visions of Excess*, 97.
3 Bataille, "The Use Value of D. A. F. de Sade," in *Visions of Excess*, 98.
4 Bataille, "The Use Value of D. A. F. de Sade," in *Visions of Excess*, 100.
5 Bataille, "The Solar Anus," in *Visions of Excess*, 6.
6 Bataille, "The Solar Anus," in *Visions of Excess*, 6.
7 Bataille, "The Solar Anus," in *Visions of Excess*, 7.
8 Bataille, "Sacrifices," in *Visions of Excess*, 133.
9 Bataille, "Sacrifices," in *Visions of Excess*, 134.
10 Bataille, "Propositions," in *Visions of Excess*, 199.

11 Bataille, "Propositions," in *Visions of Excess*, 200–201.
12 Bataille, "The Practice of Joy before Death," in *Visions of Excess*, 238.
13 Bataille, "The Sacred," in *Visions of Excess*, 241.
14 Kristeva, 248.
15 Smith, 234–235.
16 Suleiman, 325.
17 Suleiman, 326.
18 Suleiman, 315.
19 Suleiman, 318.
20 Dworkin in Suleiman, 321.
21 Sontag qtd. in Suleiman, 321.
22 Kristeva, 238
23 Kristeva, 239.
24 Suleiman qtd. in Taylor, 136.
25 Suleiman in Taylor, 136.
26 Hill, 15.
27 Hill, 15.
28 Hill, 15.
29 qtd. in Hill, 18.
30 Hill, 18.
31 Hill, 19.
32 Hill, 19.
33 Hill, 20.
34 Hill, 20.
35 Hill, 21–22.
36 Guerlac, 36.
37 Bataille, *Erotism*, 94.
38 Guerlac, 36.
39 Guerlac, 37.
40 Guerlac, 37.

41 Guerlac, 35.
42 Guerlac, 36.
43 Bataille, *Erotism*, 143–144.
44 Bataille, *Inner Experience*, 186.
45 Hill, 72.
46 Bataille, *Inner Experience*, 208.
47 Bataille, *Inner Experience*, 208.
48 Hill, 72.
49 Hill, 72.
50 Hill, 72.
51 Hill, 73.
52 Hill, 74.
53 Hill, 74–75.
54 Hill, 75
55 Hill, 75.
56 Hill, 85.
57 Hill, 92.
58 Hill, 92.
59 Hill, 93.
60 Bataille, *Inner Experience*, 170.
61 Bataille, *Inner Experience*, 171.
62 Bataille, *Inner Experience*, 177.
63 Bataille, *Inner Experience*, 181.
64 Bataille, *Inner Experience*, 187.
65 Bataille, *Inner Experience*, 187.
66 Bataille, *Inner Experience*, 192.
67 Bataille, *Inner Experience*, 194.
68 Bataille, *Inner Experience*, 199.
69 Bataille, *Inner Experience*, 174.
70 Bataille, "Sovereignty-Hegel, Death and Sacrifice," in *The Bataille Reader*, 287.

71 *The Bataille Reader*, 323.
72 *The Bataille Reader*, 325.
73 Hill, 100.
74 *The Bataille Reader*, 322–323.
75 Bataille qtd. in Igrek, 408.
76 Bataille qtd. in Igrek, 408.
77 Igrek, 410.
78 Igrek, 410.
79 Swearingen, Cutting-Gray, 9–10.
80 Swearingen, Cutting-Gray, 10.
81 Swearingen, Cutting-Gray, 10.
82 Swearingen, Cutting-Gray, 11.
83 Swearingen, Cutting-Gray, 11.
84 Swearingen, Cutting-Gray, 11.
85 Bataille, *My Mother, Madame Edwarda, The Dead Man*, 172, 168.
86 Bataille, *My Mother, Madame Edwarda, The Dead Man*, 40–41.
87 Bataille, *My Mother, Madame Edwarda, The Dead Man*, 71.
88 Bataille, *My Mother, Madame Edwarda, The Dead Man*, 117.
89 Bataille, *My Mother, Madame Edwarda, The Dead Man*, 151.
90 Bataille, *My Mother, Madame Edwarda, The Dead Man*, 158.
91 Bataille, *Story of The Eye*, 48.
92 Bataille, *Story of The Eye*, 49.
93 Bataille, *Story of The Eye*, 5.
94 Bataille, *Story of The Eye*, 5.
95 Bataille, *Story of The Eye*, 6.
96 Bataille, *Story of The Eye*, 63.

97 Bataille, *Story of The Eye*, 8.
98 Bataille, *Story of The Eye*, 21–22.
99 Bataille, *Story of The Eye*, 84.
100 Bataille, *Story of The Eye*, 45.
101 Bataille, *Divine Filth*, 38.
102 Bataille, *Divine Filth*, 17.
103 Bataille, *Divine Filth*, 39.
104 Popowski, 308–309.
105 Popowski, 310.
106 Popowski, 311.
107 Bataille, *Erotism*, 63.

VI
The Sacred/Profane or Eroticism/Ecstasy: Saint Bataille

THE SOVEREIGN SUBJECT EMBODIES THE BEST FEATURES of what is erotic, impulsively navigating the "summits—those paroxystic experiences like so many escape routes to expenditure and communication—mystic, erotica ecstatic," opposed to, yet modelled on the structure of "communal and sacramental unity."[1] Eroticism is the greatest form of energy for Bataille; it is internally complex in the subject, as well as externally transgressive in its expression. It is the pinnacle of sensual transcendence:

> The erotic moment is even the zenith of this life, in which that greatest force and the greatest intensity are revealed whenever two

> beings are attracted to each other [...] These entwined bodies, writhing and swooning, losing themselves in an excess of sensuous pleasure, are in opposition to death.[2]

The "*birth* of eroticism, out of animal sexuality," brings about "what is essential to it," he writes,[3] and in the "birth of art," humans' ability to "play" was also born as a "work that became play."[4] This connects laughter, death, and eroticism together in a kind of trinity for Bataille, and these consequentially create all forms of opposition:

> The indignity of the ape, which does not laugh [...] The complicity of the tragic—which is the basis of death—with sensual pleasure and laughter [...] The intimate opposition between the upright posture—and the anal orifice—linked to squatting.[5]

Even in the dualisms listed here, there is a sense that these oppositions allow Bataille to better examine the fundamental relationship between the sacred and profane, and further, erotic pleasure/ecstasy as they embrace this duality. He describes this basic relation as follows:

> Even after psychoanalysis, the contradictory aspects of eroticism appear in some way innumerable; their profundity is religious—it is horrible, it is tragic, it is still inadmissible. Probably all the more so because it is divine.[6]

It is "the religious meaning of eroticism" alongside of prohibition and transgression of these limits of faith that comprise a central tenet in his work, and as Dionysus is transgressive and destructive, so too is he "divine" as "the god of religious transgression."[7] He is the god "of ecstasy and madness" but his is "a restrained madness, considerate of the interests of its victims; only rarely was death the outcome" (as in the case of sacrifice for the feast).[8] In terms of this history, the decline in the cult of Dionysus was the result of a "more sober Dionysianism, a decent Dionysianism" which arose out of the "fear of derangement" of those who were faithful to Dionysus in the first century of the Roman Empire, which then perpetuated individuals converting to Christianity, argues Bataille.[9]

However, the essence of religion itself remains "subversive" because of this tension between the taboo as a limit and the transgressive event as surpassing this boundary, and even generally understood, religion "demands excess, sacrifice, and the feast, which culminates in ecstasy," he argues.[10] Christianity, in its earliest form, "attempted to liberate" the world from "eroticism," as well as advocating work over sensual pleasure, and "paradise [as] the outcome of an effort, the outcome of labor."[11] In this analysis, sacrifice remained as the "other" side of this faithful inhibition, and ecstasy accompanied these ritual practices: "An ecstasy comparable in a way to drunkenness."[12] And this "opens" up the presence of a "vexing reality, completely outside daily reality […] the *sacred*."[13]

Bataille's personal recollections regarding his possession and contemplation of the photographs the *Hundred Pieces* (1923 from George Dumas' *Traite de psychologie*), aim to assert a single and complete theory regarding the correlative relationship between "religious ecstasy and eroticism—and in particular sadism."[14] These photographs of a man being tortured to death by measured and violent acts illustrate "divine ecstasy and its opposite, extreme horror," or the religious imperative of sacrifice and suffering, as well as ecstasy and erotic transgression; offering a better fit for the abbreviated dualism of the sacred and the profane.[15] This idea of ecstasy as originating from two sources which are diametrically opposed, can be read as a consequence of Bataille's early education at the seminary at Saint-Fleur where he began studies to become a priest, a course which resulted in his rejection of Catholicism and religion more generally, and his entry into academic studies at the École des Chartes from 1918–1922. The intertwining of ecstasy with anguish created "contestation" as a primary method for Bataille, a position that Peter Connor describes as "Bataille's *fundamentum inconcussum*, his first and only 'principle of method'" which created a range of radical theories concerning inner experience.[16]

As a measure of remembrance to this past, Bataille used a series of saints to provide a foundation for a mystical and ecstatic theory, beginning with the thirteenth-century mystic, Angela of Foligno, to formulate his idea of the ecstatic. He writes the following:

> It is impossible for me to read at least most books. I don't have the desire. Too much work tires me. My nerves are shattered. I get drunk a lot. I feel faithful to life if I eat and drink what I want. Life is an enchantment, a feast, a festival: an oppressing, unintelligible dream, adorned nevertheless with a charm that I enjoy. The sentiment of chance demands that I look a difficult fate in the face. It would not be about chance if there were not an incontestable madness. I began to read, standing on a crowded train, Angela of Foligno's *Book of Visions*. I'm copying it out, not knowing how to say how fiercely I burn—the veil is torn in two, I emerge from the fog in which my impotence flails.[17]

Despite "living like a pig in the eyes of Christians," Bataille correlates his experience to Angela's, finding that "Angela surpasses him in the pursuit of abjection and ecstasy," and he states:

> I suffer from not myself burning to the point of coming close to death, so close that I inhale it like the breath of a loved being.[18]

Bataille is nonetheless ambivalent about the relationship between inner experience and mysticism, and he argues that "Angela of Foligno, speaking of God, speaks in servitude," and this permits him marking "his distance from Angela's text, insisting on the sovereignty of inner experience, which rejects any authority external to itself."[19] Nonetheless, this too is flexible or ambiguous, as he cites Angela again, claiming that, "If laughter is violent enough, there is no limit."[20]

In *The Impossible*, ecstasy/anguish is evident in two additional women saints for Bataille: Saint Catherine of Siena and Saint Teresa of Avila, and this ecstasy is one that occurs by way of suffering blood and transgression, he argues. The account of Catherine of Siena which describes how Christ's blood "which had flowed from him onto me" allows Bataille to suggest that the fragrance of the blood and her reticence to wash it away were transgressive because of the "heaviness" of the impossible and "horror" that is real in material life.[21] "Only the extremism of desire and of death enables me to attain the truth," writes Bataille as he reflects upon this ecstasy. Further, and as is true of humanity in general, the "double perspective" which composes the impossible for Bataille is first, an "excess of desire" which is "violent pleasure, horror, and death" and second, a "lack of desire."[22]

Ecstasy is best seen in Bataille's description of the "bitter lips and the eyes lost in the depths of the ceiling, swimming with ineffable happiness" as Teresa of Avila is depicted by Bernini (*The Ecstasy of Saint Teresa of Avila*).[23] In "A Story of Rats" Bataille's narrator (Aleph) drives a large nail into his lover B "to move her to anguish" in the same way that Teresa of Avila is pierced by the arrows.[24] This "dark love" is "never violent enough, never shady enough, never close enough to death," and is "utterly vulgar" as a result. Or, in comparison to these saints, Bataille sees love as the ideal vehicle for ecstasy:

> What joins me to B is the impossible, like a
> void in front of her and me, instead of a secure
> life together[25]

and he states: "we go merrily toward the abyss."[26] Even B's nakedness provides no relief from this compulsive fate: "B's nakedness, will you deliver me from anguish? But no [...] give me more anguish."[27] B's sacred and/or profane nature is demure yet vulgar, and in regards to this he writes:

> That part of the young woman between the
> mid-leg and the waist—which emphatically
> answers one's expectations—answers like the
> elusive transit of a rat. What fascinates us is
> vertiginous: sickly swells, recesses, the sewer,

like a void "of a ravine into which one is about to fall."[28] In "The Oresteia" he describes this vision of saintliness in poetic fragments and contradictions: "chance in long white stockings"[29] with "Belly open [...] head removed [...] reflection of long storm clouds [...] image of immense sky"[30] with a "halo of death."[31]

Nadia Tazi's analysis of the resurrected body as a living/dead body suggests it is both an affirmation and a negation of death as is illustrated by the demi-god, "it must don qualities that are the opposite of those it possessed on art" yet it retains these in its material presence.[32] Bodies such as those that Bataille describes as saintly, attempt to "bridge the gap between the mortal and the immortal, the human and the divine."[33] And more specifically, the "*habitus* (disposition), the *terminus* (limit) and the three dimensions compose a sexed figure" in the creation of an eventual "glorious body."[34] When this body enters "the sphere of light and purity that combines with the rational, the sublime and the sacred in that same opposition to the earthly," both the angelic and the profane figure of characters such as E, Filthy, Divinity, Simone, Marcelle, Madame Edwarda, etc., are *written* into Bataille's work as "angels" of a different order, I would argue.[35] This creates the conditions for a broader, contextual *event* by way of writing/presence:

> B's nakedness (the breasts, the hips, the fur), the torturer's toad face, the red tongue: and now, the arrows, the priest.[36]

Both his and her pain are given "some imperceptible extravagance" in the depths of ecstasy and suffering within this scene of transgression and horror, much like the *Hundred Pieces*, where a hundred deaths occur in the "dark light" of a "dawn" that is breaking in the narrator, who wonders: "what inconceivable light" is "breaking in me?"[37] The essence of martyrdom exhibited in this event reverses the idea of death, because the "summum malum, the ultimate evil," is erased by this "purification" and the "body is rid of both its flesh and the suffering it entails."[38] It is evident that Bataille describes these experiences in the passages above in the same way that Tazi does in consideration of traditional saints and their ecstatic suffering, as follows: "Floating in its charisma and basking in light, it becomes the symbol of the other world" a hagiography is created, as the "horror" of the "agony of matter and its assimilation to the spirit" via the "cult of martyrdom" uses a crucified God in the capture of a "cult of death."[39] The mystical power of the revived body is the foundation for the result of miraculous sainthood, Tazi writes:

> Having broken away from Hellenistic harmony and wrapped itself in mystery, the definition of the glorious body had to give in to practical necessities that have stressed contradiction over difference: it is only the process of spiritual elevation that is defined by degrees, mediations, anticipations.[40]

In "Dianus" Bataille's narrator again describes this joy and suffering in relation to the sacred and profane recognition of life/death where Dianus is brother and son of Diana and/or Lucifer (and Janus-faced as a result):

> The doubt born of great sorrows cannot help but illuminate those who enjoy—who can fully happiness only transfigured, in the dark halo of sorrow.[41]

The "Epilogue" concludes by describing a

> stormy, fairy-like gleam of light bathed my room: like an armed, youthful and illuminated Saint George attacking a dragon, she hurled herself at me, but the harm she intended me

was to tear off my clothes and she was armed only with a hyena's smile.[42]

For Bataille/his narrators, obscenity works to unfold the moment of true ecstasy from the commingling of the sacred and profane:

> Obscenity is itself only a form of pain, but so "lightly" linked to the sudden outpouring that, of all the pains, it is the richest, the craziest, the most worthy of envy.[43]

The "secret channels" of the obscene provide the discontinuity necessary for ecstasy.[44] Jean Starobinski's analysis finds that pain becomes "something visible—immediately transformed into something visible" when the "narrator heard the cry, noted the suffering," so pain becomes something shared, a reciprocal aesthetic relation between the sufferer and the viewer/author as we routinely see in Bataille's fiction.[45] As well, the "visible thing," the body in pain/ecstasy can be "anybody," yet this specific/generalized body is also a "*site* of a revelation—but a revelation for which it is itself the source."[46] The phenomenological expanse between this body and the narrator (or author), transfers the visible into the "visual," argues Starobinski, and in *writing* this body, the "metaphorization" of its presence and transformation

> implies an interpretation, and every interpretation involves a distance between an interpreting power and an object

> interpreted—even if that object is an event taking place in "my body."[47]

Like the basic power dynamic involved in sacrifice, this writing remains the scene of "the impossible," bringing together "violence and consciousness" by way of a sacrificial form of communication, one that expresses a "radical contestation" of conventional, religious mysticism.[48]

In denying conventional forms of mystical experience and conversion, Bataille attempted to reformulate its basic character from Christian dogma in order to reclaim some potential benefit for sovereignty and transgression, and this, in terms of upholding sacrifice and suffering (via the erotic). In a mixing of metaphors "[d]erived from the natural world," or the "traditional terminology of the mystics," such as "incandescence, flames and figuration," Bataille adds "words borrowed from technology," such as "shock, force, charge," and "a rhetoric that mixes natural cataclysms" ("sunbursts and thunder")[49] so that "the radiant bursting-forth" of the technology of death is fully described.[50] But I would argue that the relation in this formula of One-to-the-Other is perhaps too weak to sustain a balance between the sanctified and the heretical, so Bataille's *Inner Experience* becomes a negation of mysticism generally, in terms of advocating for an inner experience for the subject outside of the sacred, yet still within what could be qualified as a mystical experience.

What Bataille proposes is nothing less than the "ablation of the mystical in mysticism—a kind of secular mysticism, a mysticism without mysticism," argues

Connor.[51] Inner experience, "unlike mystical experience, yields no insight" because it belongs to "non-knowledge," but "the interiority of the experience is part of the attempt to stay the forces of meaning," and by "defending ecstasy" and "ascribing a fixed meaning" to it, the subject can appropriate this experience "for their own ends."[52] In doing this, Bataille finds himself caught up "in the very discursive network he wants to exorcize," and the shift from the "mystical" to the "inner" experience can only be strengthened by way of "absolute sovereignty" and transgression resulting from violent eroticism.[53] Where "the meaning of man is non-meaning [le non sens]," Bataille finds that eroticism intervenes to substantiate a relatively irrational system to rehabilitate the servile subject who remains alienated from his or her own self and others.[54] This discontinuity qualifies even death as a general, metaphysical event:

> If you die, it is not my death. You and I are discontinuous beings.[55]

Connor typifies Bataille's disassociation in this system, of "violence from its political causes," as a strategy that is based upon a glorification of suffering which can present itself as a "provocation," or as a

> part of a conscious will to perversity—a symptom of the bourgeois European culture in which he lived, or the expression of a profound but repressed human truth.[56]

The "disorder" of this system and/or the "representation of a disorder" in Bataille's work, is therefore, "a disorder that the mystics knew—in following the *via negativa*," they, like Bataille, were keenly aware of the "ambiguity of this human life is really that of mad laughter and of sobbing tears."[57] The individual and the social interrelate in tense and complicated ways in Bataille's texts, where the self may appear to be intact but is also porous or open to external influences, and these are forces that place limits upon, yet contain all the elements necessary for transgression in its many material forms. Texts and subjects are bounded yet unbounded in his work, quite clearly. This provides the foundation for all sensual eroticism, violence, and suffering, enabling revelation, death, and fusion as the possibility of transcendence. For Bataille, "The foundation of one's thought is the thought of another," such that

> humanity is not composed of isolated beings but of communication between them. Never are we revealed, even to ourselves, other than in a network of communication.[58]

The gulf between all living beings is the "abyss" which is the realm of not-knowingness and this as it is evident inside the space of existential anguish and elation. The "erotic tension" between subjects is a tumultuous and energetic materiality, and the way that subjectivity is constituted here is radically different from normalized accounts because the level of persistent anxiety produces a "powerful revulsion" and the body "is a potential '*menace*.'"⁵⁹ Or, alternately, it could be described as follows: "[s]omething *vile* ought to be kept to itself rather than be shared with others."⁶⁰ The conduct of such bodies in the context of "a variety of cultural expectations" intensifies the fascination and/or revulsion for the reader or narrator, and the violent outbursts of erotic energy are better seen in cultural contexts where they are constrained, and so it is that this erotic movement of energy is "destructive to the self-contained reality of interiority" as it functions to expose the subject's "fragmented, broken existence."⁶¹

Igrek argues that this subject and their fractured interiority cannot contain or possess the sacred or its counterpart, yet it remains an *indication* of both: the sacred object/act/event is what is sought out by this individual, but only in the most profane contexts. This is the pursuit of a transcendent/mystical revelation without spiritual (religious) substance for Bataille, as the fullest manifestation of heterogeneity; a state where one possesses an interiority in revolt against itself, as well as the social and cultural existence outside. This makes a possible aesthetic space which could bring cathartic relief or release (but only ideally as this rarely occurs).

Sacrifice functions doubly within this set of contradictory forces, as "both a representation of social unity and [the] concrete unleashing of violence" in response to "eternal social processes and to intrapsychic events."⁶² The sacrificial principle's goal for Bataille was to "liberate heterogeneous elements and to rupture the homogeneity of the person."⁶³ And I would argue that this is first seen in the description of "auto-mutilation" where violence is done to one's own self, and Van Gogh acts as his primary example.[64] This kind of "sacrificial mutilation" is synonymous with "sexual perversion" for Bataille, as both forms illustrate "the individual's disunity and disenchantment with the collectivity [that] finds subversive expression."[65] Therefore, the most ideal form of sacrifice represents both society's imposition of unity in an act of violence, as well as the auto-mutilator's "personal economy" which "incorporates the same violence"; and so, the social body becomes the subjective body.[66]

If we can consider violence in Sade, as in Bataille, as an *echo* of the originary moment of transgression, one that is linked to a continuum of excess and destructiveness, the textual or intellectual pleasure in ecstasy is overcome by the reality of material evil and violence. Material violence as is seen in war, comes out of "emotional states: anger, fear or desire," and collective violence, and it is "an organization of aggressive urges" which transgresses the taboo against killing but also accepts it (if fellow soldiers don't kill one another says Bataille).[67] Yet "cruelty" is a form of violent transgression of even this, as it is "not necessarily erotic" but still premeditated he argues.[68] Eroticism is the "taboo creating desire"[69] and this allows the fuller exposure of the complementary relationship of the sacred and profane, where transgression belongs to the profane, more properly.[70] Again, like the monstrous child (Gilles de Rais), Baudelaire's "poetic genius" is a desire for the "impossible," writes Bataille in *Literature and Evil*, a desire that is created by ecstasy and horror, and this "free sensibility" plays in an "atmosphere of vice, rejection and hatred," where "infinite vice" suits transgressive sovereignty.[71] That familiar dichotomy between "work versus pleasure" is "God versus Satan" for Baudelaire, writes Bataille; the productive and unproductive expenditure of energies is evident as a "rejection of God" and "the creation of a work which will survive," situates his poetry "on the path of rapid decomposition."[72]

For Sade, Bataille describes this sacred/profane dualism in the world of sacrilege versus devout faith as a central oscillation (*Justine*), or a theology of a supremely wicked Being.[73] In the Sadean universe, the love of evil which accompanies an individual's acceptance of being condemned by the Good (God), characterizes his libertines and literature, as both attempted to make evil "desirable" yet failed to fully "condemn or justify it" argues Bataille.[74] The intelligibility of violence in Sade remains unintelligible because of its banality, and the tornadic effect of his violent narratives. Bataille argues that "the objects of desire are invariably propelled towards torture and death"[75] and the libertines who are "splendid and violent,"[76] are also uncontrolled and frenzied in their desires as representations of the contradiction between the profane and the sacred.[77] Like the suffering of the saints, but without the origin of their rapture from a conventional, religious source, "Sexual disorder discomposes the coherent forms which establish" these libertines and "moves them into an infinity which is death."[78]

Finally, as is true for Jean Genet, a commitment to "supreme Evil" is only sought out of a commitment to "supreme Good" argues Bataille.[79] Genet, he finds, is only sovereign in "Evil," and the "impasse of unlimited transgression" is caused by an *excess of sin*.[80] This remains a "failed sovereignty"[81] says Bataille, because of Genet's "inability to communicate"[82] and therefore, he was a "condemned creature of society by way of this basic duality between Good and Evil."[83] The "cold and fragile quality in Genet's writing" is comparatively easy to make by analogy to the corpse, a dead body/text with a fleeting or insubstantial "grimace" concludes Bataille.[84] For Bataille, Sade's work was truthful, as it

> contains the bad news of a conciliation between the living and that which kills them, between Good and Evil […] between the loudest cry and silence.[85]

Yet Bataille cautions us not to read Sade "literally" or "seriously," because Sade's elaboration of "a theology of the supremely wicked Being" only substitutes God with Nature "in a state of perpetual motion."[86] And even in the most sovereign author or subject, Bataille finds that contradictions exist between advocating for, yet denying evil: "What is good or evil" for Sade is *unknown* because we can't "analyze the laws of nature and your heart" as Sade writes.[87] The idea of the profane world was central to Sade's metaphysics, both in the broad, indifferent movement of the Universe and its laws, as well as the "human heart." In this, Bataille suggests that "we talk about him, admire him, but nobody feels that he should be like him," because "we dream of other 'terrors.'"[88] Sade's *inexhaustible* enterprise of textual violence, sexual performance, and extermination, presents the reader with a perpetuation of natural crime that is the energy which moves the profane Universe. Why bother to develop a character when you can kill them off, and evil is the operative device to use for such closure. This is offered as a cure for the boredom of the sacred, perhaps, but also for the profane.

> Boredom seeps from the monstrosity of Sade's work, but it is this very boredom which constitutes its significance.[89]

The violent *mystery* around such evil, makes evil become evident in the "incompatibility between violence, which is blind, and the lucidity of consciousness."[90] The "disorder and excess" of the basic "condition of evil" in texts like *120 Days of Sodom* offers the remainder of the ruin of numerous pieces of the profane and brutal world:

> amputated fingers, the eyes, the torn finger nails, the tortures of which moral horror intensifies the pain, the mother induced, by cunning and terror, to murder her son, the cries, the blood and the stench

are all a "blasphemy," argued Bataille.[91] This profane materiality becomes actualized in the evil "consciousness" that looks to liberate itself outside of the text (possibly), but is prevented from doing so; its "powerlessness" comes to qualify its singular performativity *only* within the text.[92] If, as Bataille argues, Sade's "system is the ruinous form of eroticism," this must be the one aspect of the duality of the profane and sacred, acting like a "blind" sovereign power based on "denial," transgression, and violence, and therefore, evil cannot recuperate any mystical or ecstatic illumination.[93]

The apathy of the libertines' criminal desire, as we also see (to a degree) in Bataille's characters in *Story of The Eye*, extends only to the doorstep of the profane world, yet it is situated (or hopes for) the possibility of release that is only offered inside the sphere of the sacred. The literary performance of evil in these texts suggests that "no evil is possible" for "man in his entirety," because satisfaction and pleasure in hurting others suspends the idea of evil as being absolute, argues Bataille. The libertines gain satisfaction in these arenas of transgression, and they speak only to "their own kind," indulging "in long speeches to show they are right" so they can argue that they are "obeying the dictates of Nature."[94] The "use value of excrement" in these diatribes is textual and performative for Bataille, and the principle which guides this is "the violent excretion of the sexual object coinciding with a powerful or tortured ejaculation."[95] Eroticism, under the conditions of the profane text/world, only moves downward, whereas the inclusion of the sacred asks that such erotic violence and suffering rise upwards so that a mystical or ecstatic release can occur. Yet, the dynamic between Good and Evil, Saints and Sinners, Crime and the Moral Good, are still fixed in suspended animation in that basic figuration of the profane and the sacred.

Bataille's first publication, *Notre-Dame de Rheims* (1918), was an exposition of the "ideological system its architecture represents" and this is something that

Bataille worked to reject in the following ten years of his life, so that

> the young author who once attempted a kind of textual reconstructing of the bombed cathedral […] was by his late twenties abandoning it to its destruction.

Still, he continued to struggle with these same thematic issues in his subsequent work, as both an invalidation: to "reduce [it] to zero, erase," as well as a "tribute to the immense symbolic power of the cathedral."[96] This kind of duality can be seen in his descriptions of Quarr Abbey on the Isle of Wight, where "[t]wo worlds are mingled in the complex architecture" of the Abbey to illustrate a mystical space versus a "profane […] illumination" which is primary for inner experience itself.[97] For Bataille, the cathedral and the Abbey are

> the expression of the true nature of societies, as physiognomy is the expression of the nature of individuals […] thus the great monuments rise up like dams, opposing a logic of majesty and authority to all unquiet elements; it is in the form of cathedrals and palaces that church and state speak to and impose silence upon the crowds.[98]

The idea of "closed beings" that are changed by way of a "loss of identity," and this because of the ventures of sin, is what Pierre Klossowski contrasts with Bataille's opposition to the "opening of beings," which makes evil and good "indiscernible." He grounds this in Bataille's descriptions of the deficiency or lack of/in language to represent the constituent parts of such identity: loss, compensation, desire, and he concludes that "One is forced to open notions beyond themselves."[99] For Klossowski, this cannot be anything but a Heideggerian and metaphysical kind of opening, a "preoccupation" concerning the "contents of experience" and discontinuity with these, but always by way of a nihilistic set of philosophical inquiries.[100] The "ontological catastrophe" of this thinking is Bataille's

> reverse side of a zenith reached in what he calls sovereign moments: intoxication, laughter, erotic and sacrificial effusion, experiences characterized by an expenditure without compensation, a lavishness without measure, a destruction void of meaning, goal, and utility.[101]

This discontinuity produces "revolt" against the "world of work and presupposition,"[102] but this seems superficial argues Klossowski, as he asks "how could laughter be comparable to ecstasy or erotic effusion?"[103] Similarly, the reversal of ecstasy occurs when it is recognized as a "sovereign moment": but in doing this, reveals itself "to be a simulacrum of death" more directly and keenly.[104] "Ecstasy," he writes is "powerless," as "there persists in ecstasy a sort of constant consciousness of ecstasy, placing it on the level of things proposed for ownership" and the object that becomes appropriated, is only "an object of instruction."[105] The radical transformation of the subject who is *closed* must precede and support this sovereignty and its dichotomous conception of the world, but not by way of mere atheism, as Klossowski argues but rather, a time when "the vacancy of the self responding to the vacancy of God would constitute the sovereign moment," or what would be the final destruction of the duality of the sacred and the profane.[106]

Notes

1. Besnier, 21.
2. Bataille, *The Tears of Eros*, 33.
3. Bataille, *The Tears of Eros*, 39.
4. Bataille, *The Tears of Eros*, 47.
5. Bataille, *The Tears of Eros*, 53.
6. Bataille, *The Tears of Eros*, 69.
7. Bataille, *The Tears of Eros*, 71.
8. Bataille, *The Tears of Eros*, 74.
9. Bataille, *The Tears of Eros*, 77.
10. Bataille, *The Tears of Eros*, 72.
11. Bataille, *The Tears of Eros*, 78.
12. Bataille, *The Tears of Eros*, 199.
13. Bataille, *The Tears of Eros*, 199.
14. Bataille, *The Tears of Eros*, 206.
15. Bataille, *The Tears of Eros*, 207.
16. Connor, 69.
17. Bataille qtd. in Hollywood, 220–221.
18. Bataille qtd. in Hollywood, 221.
19. Hollywood, 221.

20 Bataille qtd. in Hollywood, 221.
21 Bataille, *The Impossible*, 10.
22 Bataille, *The Impossible*, 53.
23 Bataille, *The Impossible*, 22.
24 Bataille, *The Impossible*, 16.
25 Bataille, *The Impossible*, 19.
26 Bataille, *The Impossible*, 20.
27 Bataille, *The Impossible*, 29.
28 Bataille, *The Impossible*, 38.
29 Bataille, *The Impossible*, 122.
30 Bataille, *The Impossible*, 126.
31 Bataille, *The Impossible*, 127.
32 Tazi, 532.
33 Tazi, 534.
34 Tazi, 535.
35 Tazi, 542–543.
36 Bataille, *The Impossible*, 48.
37 Bataille, *The Impossible*, 96.
38 Tazi, 543.
39 Tazi, 544–546.
40 Tazi, 548.
41 Bataille, *The Impossible*, 116.
42 Bataille, *The Impossible*, 117.
43 Bataille, *The Impossible*, 116.
44 Bataille, *Erotism*, 23.
45 Starobinski, 384.
46 Starobinski, 384.
47 Starobinski, 386.
48 Irwin, 127.
49 Bataille, *Visions of Excess*, 200.
50 Connor, 93.

51 Connor, 55.
52 Connor, 56.
53 Connor, 57.
54 Bataille, *Inner Experience*, 172.
55 Bataille, *Erotism*, 18–19.
56 Connor, 162.
57 Bataille, *The Tears of Eros*, 20.
58 Bataille, *Literature and Evil*, 310.
59 Igrek, 413.
60 Igrek, 413.
61 Igrek, 414.
62 Irwin, 2.
63 *The Bataille Reader*, 269.
64 *The Bataille Reader*, 270.
65 *The Bataille Reader*, 275–276.
66 Irwin, 10.
67 Bataille, *Erotism*, 64.
68 Bataille, *Erotism*, 79.
69 Bataille, *Erotism*, 72.
70 Bataille, *Erotism*, 67.
71 Bataille, *Literature and Evil*, 31–32.
72 Bataille, *Literature and Evil*, 42.
73 Bataille, *Literature and Evil*, 89.
74 Bataille, *Literature and Evil*, 90
75 Bataille, *Literature and Evil*, 94–95.
76 Bataille, *Literature and Evil*, 96.
77 Bataille, *Literature and Evil*, 98.
78 Bataille, *Literature and Evil*, 99.
79 Bataille, *Literature and Evil*, 151.
80 Bataille, *Literature and Evil*, 159.
81 Bataille, *Literature and Evil*, 166.

82 Bataille, *Literature and Evil*, 167.
83 Bataille, *Literature and Evil*, 168.
84 Bataille, *Literature and Evil*, 169.
85 Bataille, *Literature and Evil*, 88.
86 Bataille, *Literature and Evil*, 89.
87 qtd. in Bataille, *Literature and Evil*, 90.
88 Bataille, *Literature and Evil*, 93.
89 Bataille, *Literature and Evil*, 94.
90 Bataille, *Literature and Evil*, 89.
91 Bataille, *Literature and Evil*, 99.
92 Bataille, *Literature and Evil*, 103.
93 Bataille, *Erotism*, 171.
94 Bataille, *Erotism*, 188.
95 Bataille, "The Use Value of D. A. F. de Sade," in *Visions of Excess*, 92.
96 Connor, 23.
97 Connor, 23–24.
98 Bataille qtd. in Lahiji, 128.
99 Bataille qtd. in Klossowski, 149–150.
100 Klossowski, 150.
101 Klossowski, 151.
102 Klossowski, 152.
103 Klossowski, 153.
104 Klossowski, 153.
105 Klossowski, 154.
106 Klossowski, 154.

VII
A Conclusion for Bataille and the Anti-Aesthetic

BATAILLE'S AMBITIOUS REWRITING OF BOTH philosophy and literature occurred at a time when the certainty of Modernity had become disheveled, leaving ideal concepts of the Subject, as well as the moral community in question. This is something that follows Nietzsche's Zarathrustran declaration of the death of God when "The universal god destroys rather than supports the human aggregations that raise his ghost,"[1] leaving an "inconceivable void" that becomes labyrinthine in its structure.[2] As an experiential, phenomenological, and transgressive refusal of modern certainty, Bataille's work was a response to the theories, thinkers, and structures of his period which supported this claim, offering provocative and deconstructive critiques to counter the decay of the subject in the Modern age.

The showcasing of transgression offers an alternative aesthetic order to that of the traditional philosophers such as Kant or Schopenhauer, and instead, the framing of heterogeneous power within a system of excess and expenditure or the economy of restriction, allows for a sovereign freedom and this, by way of his literature. But as well, the reformation of Kant's parergon arose out of Bataille's "economic" perspective as something like a "'left' artistic margin" or the "sur": what is "marginalized or minimized within the text of philosophy" to "exceed the center."[3] His writing, both philosophical and literary, embodied "an implementation of transgressing" but was also "heterogeneous detritus which deconstructs" all systems of homogeneity.[4]

Like all his work, a theory of aesthetic value is positioned as an Other to any other proposed structure. As a reflection of the way Modernity is an Other to the postmodern, Bataille's aesthetic is therefore a kind of representation of a new (renewed) order, a "reduction to pure difference" where transgression functions "as that which reaffirms the re-reproduction and circulation of the hyperreal" as it becomes "stretched across consciousness into the realm of the body."[5] And at its "heart" is the countering of knowledge with "un-knowledge" as it appears in the "economic" or "productive."[6] The "non-economic" economy proposed in the *Accursed Share* is an "economy of the beautiful art and genius" worked out by way of "a radical prohibition of exchange," and the resulting "aesthetic economy" or "economimesis" as Derrida argues, correlates "waste and taste" versus the Kantian system in the "Third Critique," reconstructing the earlier aesthetic order by correlating these two "in the labyrinths of the general economy."[7] This "deconstruction of taste and disgust" are given by Bataille as the "restricted effects" of this anti-aesthetic and Arkady Plotnitsky argues that even Derrida's analysis of "economimesis" is therefore dependent, "fundamentally on Bataille's conceptions" in this assertion of an oppositional aesthetic form.[8] As Plotnitsky asserts: "the economy of every account—literary, philosophical or other—is always already a general economy" for Bataille.

The general economy of the body acts as the immanent ground of excess/desire and aesthetic experience for Bataille, or at least it must be considered as such I argue, as it possesses and enacts the excretions and operations of jouissance, and this by way of perversion as something that is articulate, and material, so therefore, open to interpretation or alternately, opposed to this very act. Bataille's concept of the labyrinth takes up this material form in order to provide a complex refutation of theory, alone. It is the "contradictory movements of degradation and growth" that "in the diffuse development of human existence," provide "a bewildering complexity" he writes.[9] The "*principle of insufficiency*" is what guides all manner of development for Bataille, and this provides the means to maintain uncertainty in being and in the labyrinth, in terms of the loss of meaning that occurs there.[10] The internal structures of the body afford a material set of examples of labyrinthine systems, and as well, a broader physiological and biological economy I would argue. And waste as the remains of consumption, digestion, and expulsion in this system, indicate that the body is the foundation for an anti-aesthetic theory of this insufficiency; the bowels, bladder, vagina, ear, mouth, throat, brain, all can be aesthetically understood as a material/immaterial labyrinth. The radical support for materialism he finds in the excess or the refuse of the body supplies Bataille with any number of oppositional principles. And this creates the "sovereign operation of Bataille's disease, consumption" and transgression, as a waste without aim.[11]

The renegotiation of the material body into something akin to the "Body Without Organs," as it firsts appeared in Antonin Artaud's writing can be examined as a counterpart to the deterministic and metaphysical account that Bataille's philosophy offers. The similar transgressive (and excessive) framing of this body in literature and philosophy via an anti-aesthetics allows this, I would suggest. As well, in Artaud, like Bataille, the characterization of its origin from an impulse of psychic violence in the "reinvention in the face of a continual experience of the dissolution of identity," allowed for a radical Body to emerge.[12] Both Artaud and Bataille's work sought a new aesthetic through a form of philosophical consecration with this Body. In conjunction with an adoption of Nietzsche's Apollonian and Dionysian creation/destruction, this Body fueled its inception, and what was created was a doubling of negation and creation that could only be known from its "most profane spaces," either in defeat or excitation: "between the slat and the ceiling" for Artaud,[13] or the "tiny particle of dazzling light" that "springs from an accumulation of refuse" in "the bottom of a well" for Bataille.[14]

In the realm of this excess and degradation there is an "organless" and immaculate body that emerges, and like Artaud, Bataille's new body is "a true body, one that had overcome "the glamour that organs cast on man to bind themselves more closely to him," in order to become organless made up of "all bone and nerve," like "a walking tree of will." But never moving as far as Artaud, or to the point of erasing sexuality and desire, Bataille, instead, moved this Body into the uninhibited region of sovereign calculation which retains a fixation on the "oral, anal, and genital."[15] For Artaud, like Nietzsche, the human must move past the notion of God and biological design, and while Bataille holds to a great part of this, he did not absolutely reject God, as he reforms him instead: "God is a whore, exactly like all other whores."[16] And the most perfect whore/God is Madame Edwarda, whose body occupies the entire space or frame of the short story by her own admission: "'You can see for yourself,' she said, 'I'm GOD',"[17] while she shows the narrator her genitalia, and after this disclosure he says:

> I say of Madame Edwarda that she is GOD. But GOD figured as a public whore and gone crazy.[18]

For Bataille, "sovereign action" does not accord with the "physics of power" upon which the project of Modernity and certainty rests, and since no particular logic governs this sovereign experience, its "model of action" is based on a material form; the

> unveiled body, the stiff, which is a negation of
> my body and which forces the double negation
> of my body.[19]

This is the "encoding of women" that occurs in Bataille's fiction, and the "materialism" of the body is, in addition, the limit of philosophy's "consciousness and the philosophy of language."[20] These combine to provoke a different aesthetic order, one where "visions of excess are visions of the body and visions of death" argues Haase.[21] For these women and their bodies, the heterogeneous, the transgressive, and the sovereign act as the main elements of a fluidity and philosophical exegesis I would argue. Like "the exterior beauty of flowers is besmirched by hideous yet central sex organs which, when uncovered, reveal themselves as rather sordid tufts," so too do the women in Bataille's fiction provide aesthetic relief by way of their conventional beauty, but always in opposition to their grotesque desires and perverse excess.[22] Beauty is a core component of any aesthetic system, and the doubled effect of beauty and/or ugliness provides a more complex theory of aesthetic and material presence in Bataille's work. The "naïveté of the philosopher accounting for beautiful art" is what Bataille laughs at, and his "laughter would in fact be most 'logical' here" writes Plotnitsky.[23] Bataille correlates beauty with sacrifice, where the sacrificial victim is chosen by way of an ideal of beauty, so the "full brutality of death" can become visible in the act of extermination of such beauty.[24] Additionally, writes Bataille, beauty "is desired in order that it may be befouled; not for its own sake, but for the joy brought by the certainty of profaning it."²⁵

This transgressive aesthetic utilizes an alternative concept of beauty from a prior ideation, and this is always identifiable as a woman, so it is first, this specific claim by Bataille:

> How sweet it is to gaze long upon the object of our desire, instead of dying by going the whole way, by yielding to the excessive violence of desire!²⁶

And next, seen in this more particular description: "in speaking of the beauty of a woman," one must avoid "referring to beauty in general," and only refer to "the function of beauty in eroticism."²⁷ For a greater aesthetic manifestation and appreciation of such a woman, everything that belongs to the animal must be hidden because "any suggestion of the animal in the human form is unquestionably repugnant," however, the primacy of the erotic seems to prevent a disinterested aesthetic appreciation of this, nonetheless.²⁸ This is the most evident, material form of aesthetic transgression, and it is inherently anti-aesthetic if one accepts a traditional set of approaches to aesthetic theory to be valid: disinterest, objectivity, and standardized criteria, and in opposition to this: the "pervert" in this aesthetic system would appear as "both below and beyond the level of "individuals" which are the norm. In Bataille's work, characters like Pierre (*ME*) present "an arbitrary subordination of the habitual life functions to one sole insubordinate function, a craving for an improper object," and this by way of his ability to open "a broader perspective, that of sensuous polymorphy."[29] This perversity occurs by way of what Klossowski describes as first, a "morose delectation" in Sade; one that

> consists in that movement of the soul by which it bears itself voluntarily towards images of forbidden carnal or spiritual acts in order to linger in contemplation of them [...] spontaneous revery.[30]

And in this anti-aesthetic, which is well-suited to examine Bataille's works with their first-person narrators, "consciousness abandons itself to the slow work of dissolution by the dark forces" concludes Klossowski of Sade, as I do of Bataille.[31]

In Sarah Wilson's analysis of the relationship between Bataille and artist Jean Fautrier in the 1940s, she correlates the visual art of Fautrier with the works of Bataille, and it is clear in this association that "the metaphysical became conjoined to the erotic," where Fautrier's "disturbing" nudes illustrate the "encounter with the Sacred" from Bataille's *Madame Edwarda* as their inspiration.[32] This can also be considered in regards to the association between Hans Bellmer's work and Bataille's. Nonetheless, in conjunction with Bataille's "rewriting" of the novel or essay, Fautrier's "reinforming" of the conventional visual representation of the body as "nature morte," or depictions of "slaughter and evisceration," indicated that he was moving, like Bataille, "towards the painting of the wound."³³ She describes this as follows:

> Now the painting itself became "all wound," like the body of Bataille's Chinese torture victim: the exposure of the viscera expressed a condition of "life in death."³⁴

In a full representation of the anti-aesthetic situatedness of Bataille's work, "Fautrier's art is a majestic supplement to the erotic and terrible universe of Bataille" because it composes and reconstitutes the world "of inner experience" as a "rupture" by way of a radical reinterpretation of the body, desire, transgression, and finally, death.³⁵

In conclusion, this introduction to Bataille's work has gravitated around the aesthetic and comprehensive character of his philosophy and literature, retaining an interdisciplinary perspective of critical curiosity, and as well, a thorough deconstructive analysis of the boundaries between world and Subject, the sacred and profane, ecstasy and anguish, art and sovereignty, and these as they are fixed within, and originate out of the impossible. The "aesthetic field" or the anti-aesthetic movement that underlies Bataille's work more generally is a "plural" one, it is a "stratified ensemble—from Kant and Hegel, to Nietzsche" one that provides a set of transformations that are given as a "plural style" or a "landscape" of the anti-aesthetic.³⁶ I would close by asserting that Bataille's positon as an *Other* to all conventional knowledge and practice allows the possibility for the reader's entrance into his work, and this occurs, routinely, because of the aesthetic (and not), the possible (and not), and all the other dualities that are the foundation of his work, where the reader can lose and yet find herself in Bataille's *labyrinth*.

Notes

1. Bataille, *Visions of Excess*, 175.
2. Derrida, "Tympan," 157 n. 9.
3. Plotnitsky, 109.
4. Haase, 127.
5. Haase, 130.
6. Plotnitsky, 109–110.
7. Plotnitsky, 118–119.
8. Plotnitsky, 121.
9. Bataille, *Visions of Excess*, 171.
10. Bataille, *Visions of Excess*, 172–173.
11. Plotnitsky, 119.
12. Artaud, 86.
13. Artaud, 102.
14. Bataille, *The Impossible*, 133.
15. Eshleman in Artaud, 34–35.
16. Bataille, *Erotism*, 269.
17. Bataille, *My Mother*, 150.
18. Bataille, *My Mother*, 155.
19. Haase, 136.
20. Haase, 138.
21. Haase, 140.
22. Haase, 127.

23 Haase, 123.
24 Bataille, *Erotism*, 144.
25 Bataille, *Erotism*, 144.
26 Bataille, *Erotism*, 141–142.
27 Bataille, *Erotism*, 142.
28 Bataille, *Erotism*, 143.
29 Klossowski, 23.
30 Klossowski, 113.
31 Klossowski, 114.
32 Wilson, 174.
33 Wilson, 174–177.
34 Wilson, 177.
35 Wilson, 187.
36 Plotnitsky, 126.

Bibliography

Artaud, Antonin. *Watchfiends and Rackscreams*. Translated and edited by Clayton Eshleman. London: Exact Change, 2004.

Bataille, Georges. *Literature and Evil*. Translated by Alastair Hamilton. London: Calder and Boyars, 1973.

—. *Visions of Excess: Selected Writings 1927–1939*. Edited by Alan Stoekl. Minneapolis: University of Minnesota Press, 1985.

—. *Erotism: Death and Sensuality*. Translated by Mary Dalwood. San Francisco: City Lights Books, 1986.

—. *Story of the Eye*. Translated by Joachim Neugroschel. San Francisco: City Lights Books, 1987.

—. *Inner Experience*. Translated by Leslie Anne Boldt. Albany: State University of New York Press, 1988.

—. *The Tears of Eros*. Translated by Peter Connor. San Francisco: City Light Books, 1989.

—. *The Accursed Share: Volume 1*. Translated by Robert Hurley. New York: Zone Books, 1991.

—. *The Trial of Gilles de Rais*. Translated by Richard Robinson. Los Angeles: Amok Books, 1991.

—. *The Bataille Reader*. Edited by Fred Botting and Scott Wilson. London: Blackwell, 1997.

—. *My Mother, Madame Edwarda, The Dead Man*. Translated by Austryn Wainhouse. London: Marion Boyars Publishers, 2003.

—. *Divine Filth: Lost Writings by Georges Bataille*. Translated and edited by Mark Spitzer. London: Creation Books, 2004.

—. *Theory of Religion*. Translated by Robert Hurley. New York: Zone Books, 1989.

Bailey Gill, Carolyn. "Introduction." In *Bataille: Writing the Sacred*, xv–xix. London: Routledge, 1995.

Benveniste, Émile. "Gift and Exchange in the Indo-European Vocabulary." In *The Logic of the Gift*, edited by Alan D. Schrift, 33–42. New York: Routledge, 1997.

Besnier, Jean-Michel. "Bataille, the Emotive Intellectual." In *Bataille: Writing the Sacred*, 12–25. London: Routledge, 1995.

Bourdieu, Pierre. "Marginalia—Some Additional Notes on the Gift." In *The Logic of the Gift*, edited by Alan D. Schrift, 234–238. New York: Routledge, 1997.

Breton, André. *Mad Love*. Translated by Mary Ann Caws. Lincoln: University of Nebraska Press, 1987.

Caws, Mary Ann. *The Eye in the Text*. Princeton: Princeton University Press, 1981.

Connor, Peter. *Georges Bataille and the Mysticism of Sin*. Baltimore: John Hopkins University Press, 2003.

Deleuze, Gilles. *Sacher-Masoch: An Interpretation*. Translated by Jean McNeil. London: Faber and Faber, 1971.

Derrida, Jacques. "Différance" and "Tympan." In *A Derrida Reader: Between the Blinds*, edited by Peggy Kamuf. New York: Columbia University Press, 1991.

Fer, Briony. "Poussiére/peinture: Bataille on Painting." In *Bataille: Writing the Sacred*, edited by Carolyn Bailey Gill, 154–171. London: Routledge, 1995.

Gallop, Jane. *Intersections: A Reading of Sade with Bataille, Blanchot, and Klossowski*. Lincoln: University of Nebraska Press, 1981.

Gasché, Rodolphe. "Heliocentric Exchange." In *The Logic of the Gift*, edited by Alan D. Schrift, 100–121. New York: Routledge, 1997.

Goldhammer, Jesse. *The Headless Republic: Sacrificial Violence in Modern French Thought*. Ithaca, NY: Cornell University Press, 2005.

Guerlac, Suzanne. *Literary Polemics: Bataille, Sartre, Valéry, Breton*. Stanford: Stanford University Press, 1997.

Haase, Andrew. "Body Shops: The Death of Georges Bataille." In *Body Invaders: Panic Sex in America*, edited by Arthur and Marilouise Kroker, 120–149. Montreal: New World Perspectives, 1987.

Hill, Leslie. *Bataille, Klossowski, Blanchot: Writing at the Limit*. London: Oxford University Press, 2001.

Hollywood, Amy. "'Beautiful As a Wasp': Angela of Foligno and Georges Bataille." *Harvard Theological Review*, 92, no. 2 (April 1999): 219–236.

Igrek, Apple Zefelius. "Violence and Heterogeneity," *Janus Head* 7, no. 2 (2004): 404–428.

Irwin, Alexander. *Saints of the Impossible*. Minneapolis: University of Minnesota Press, 2002.

Klossowski, Pierre. *Sade My Neighbor*. Translated by Alphonso Lingis. Evanston, IL: Northwestern University Press, 1991.

Kristeva, Julia. "Bataille, Experience, Practice." In *On Bataille: Critical Essays*, edited by Leslie Boldt-Irons, 237–264. Albany: State University of New York Press, 1995.

Lahiji, Nadir. "The Gift of Time: Le Corbusier Reading Bataille." In *Surrealism and Architecture*, edited by Thomas Mical, 119–122. New York: Taylor and Francis, 2004.

Lechte, John. "Surrealism and the Practice of Writing." In *Bataille: Writing the Sacred*, edited by Carolyn Bailey Gill, 117–132. London: Routledge, 1995.

MacKendrick, Karmen. *Counterpleasures*. Albany: State University of New York Press, 1999.

Matthews, J. H. *Towards the Poetics of Surrealism*. New York: Syracuse University Press, 1976.

Nietzsche, Friedrich. *Hammer of the Gods*. London: Creation Books, 1996.

Piel, Jean. "Bataille and the World from 'The Notion of Expenditure' to *The Accursed Share*." In *On Bataille: Critical Essays*, edited by Leslie Boldt-Irons, 95–106. Albany: State University of New York, 1995.

Plotnitsky, Arkady. "The Maze of Taste: On Bataille, Derrida, and Kant." *On Bataille: Critical Essays*, edited by Leslie Boldt-Irons, 107–127. Albany: State University of New York Press, 1995.

Popowski, Mikhal H. "On the Eye of Legibility: Illegibility in George Bataille's Story of the Eye." In *On Bataille: Critical Essays*, edited by Leslie Boldt-Irons,

295–311. Albany: State University of New York, 1995.

Rubin Suleiman, Susan. "Transgression and the Avant-Garde." In *On Bataille: Critical Essays*, edited by Leslie Boldt-Irons, 313–333. Albany: State University of New York Press, 1995.

Smith, Paul. "Bataille's Erotic Writings and the Return of the Subject." In *On Bataille: Critical Essays*, edited by Leslie Boldt-Irons, 233–236. Albany: State University of New York Press, 1995.

Starobinski, Jean. "The Natural and Literary History of Bodily Sensation." In *Fragments for a History of the Human Body: Part Two*, edited by Michael Feher, Ramona Naddaff, and Nadia Tazi, 350–370. New York: Zone Books, 1989.

Stoekl, Allan. "Bataille, Gift Giving, and the Cold War." In *The Logic of the Gift*. Edited by Alan D. Schrift, 245–254. New York: Routledge, 1997.

Swearingen, James E., and Joanne Cutting-Gray. *Extreme Beauty: Aesthetics, Politics, Death*. New York: Continuum Books, 2002.

Taylor, Sue. *Hans Bellmer: The Anatomy of Anxiety*. New York: MIT Press, 2002.

Tazi, Nadia. "Celestial Bodies: A Few Stops on the Way to Heaven." In *Fragments for a History of the Human Body: Part Two*, edited by Michael Feher, Ramona Naddaff, and Nadia Tazi, 518–552. New York: Zone Books, 1989.

Credits

Cover image: The Ecstasy of Saint Theresa by Giancarlo Bernini. Church of Santa Maria della Vittoria, Rome. 1647–1652. Credit to Alvesgaspar <https://en.wikipedia.org/wiki/File:Ecstasy_of_Saint_Teresa_September_2015-2a.jpg>. Edited by Kısmet Press, and republished under the original Creative Commons license: Creative Commons Attribution-Share Alike 4.0 International license.

Frontispiece: Ecstasy of Saint Teresa by Giuseppe Bazzani. 1745–1750. Oil on canvas, 76 x 60 cm. Szépmûvészeti Múzeum, Budapest. <https://commons.wikimedia.org/wiki/File:Giuseppe_Bazzani_-_The_Ecstasy_of_St_Therese_-_WGA01527.jpg>. Image in the public domain; edited by Kısmet Press.

This short introduction to Georges Bataille's work examines his philosophy and literature by identifying the central theories of transgression, sovereignty and/or subjectivity, sacrifice, art and/or aesthetic radicalism, general and restricted economies, as well as the profane and the sacred by way of eroticism and ecstasy. Bataille remains a singular and complex figure, an Outsider in poststructuralist, continental philosophy, and the complexities of his interdisciplinary approach to literature and theory compels this introduction to explore and explain his innovative and often controversial work as an impossible philosopher, as well as a philosopher of the Impossible.

Dr. Lynn Hughey Engelbert teaches philosophy at the University of Alberta and Athabasca University in Alberta, Canada. She has published essays on avant-garde philosophers and artists, and is concerned with postmodern aesthetics more generally. She is currently working on a book about the feminist sublime and its connection to Gilles Deleuze and Felix Guattari.

www.ingramcontent.com/pod-product-compliance
Lightning Source LLC
Chambersburg PA
CBHW052134010526
44113CB00036B/2198